PIE Manual

PIE Manual

Person-in-Environment System

*The PIE Classification System for
Social Functioning Problems*

By James M. Karls and Karin E. Wandrei

NASW PRESS

National Association of Social Workers
Washington, DC

Ann A. Abbott, PhD, ACSW, *President*
Sheldon R. Goldstein, ACSW, LISW, *Executive Director*

First impression, September 1994
Second impression, November 1995
Third impression, August 1996
Fourth impression, October 1997
Fifth impression, January 1999
Sixth impression, May 2001

© 1994 by the NASW Press

Library of Congress Cataloging-in-Publication Data

Karls, James M., 1927–
    PIE manual : person-in-environment system : the PIE classification system for social functioning problems / by James M. Karls and Karin E. Wandrei.
        p.   cm.
    Includes bibliographical references.
    ISBN 0-87101-254-5 (alk. paper)
    1. Person-in-environment system.   I. Wandrei, Karin Evon.
II. Title.
HV43.5.K37   1994
361.1′014—dc20
                                                                        94-34762
                                                                        CIP

Printed in the United States of America

Contents

Introduction vii

Chapter 1   Structure of the PIE System 1

Chapter 2   Use of the Manual 3

Chapter 3   Factor I: Social Role Functioning 7

Chapter 4   Factor II: Person in Environment/
Problems in the Environment 23

Chapter 5   Severity, Duration, and Coping Indexes 35

Chapter 6   Case Examples Using PIE in
Various Agency Settings 38

Chapter 7   The Mini-PIE 49

Appendix A   Training Social Workers in the Use of PIE 58

Appendix B   Social Work Interventions 64

Introduction

The *PIE Manual* is intended for the use of social work and other human services practitioners, as well as educators, administrators, and researchers. PIE is a tool for describing, classifying, and recording the social functioning problems presented by the clients of social workers. The system is designed to accommodate not only varied practice settings but also the various theoretical orientations that guide the practice of social workers and other human services practitioners.

The PIE system calls first for a social work assessment that is then translated to a description and coding of the client's problems in social functioning. Problems in social functioning are identified in terms of social role performance. These social role problems are influenced by problems in the society or community in which the client lives, what is referred to in this manual as "the environment." Social functioning is a client's ability to accomplish the activities necessary for daily living (for example, obtaining food, shelter, and transportation) and to fulfill major social roles as required by the client's subculture or community.

Although the PIE system produces a descriptive statement and coding of social role and environmental problems, it also requires the social worker to pay attention to client strengths. To accomplish this, a Coping Index is used (along with a Severity and Duration Index) to note the client's ability to deal with the presenting problem. The practitioner should be aware of the client's positive social role functioning and the positive environmental conditions that will facilitate intervention with the client.

Social work intervention is sought or is appropriate when role performance becomes a problem either to the potential client or to others or when environmental problems negatively affect social functioning.

In its present form this manual is limited to the description of the social functioning problems of individuals age 18 and older. For practitioners working with children, the manual will be useful for describing the problems of the adults in a child's life. Practitioners working with families can use the manual to describe the social functioning problems of individual adults in the family and to help analyze the interactional problems in the family structure.

I.

Structure of the PIE System

PIE provides a systematic approach to assessing the social functioning problems experienced by the clients of social workers. When used in agency practice, it can produce problem descriptions that are concise, uniform, and easily understood by both clients and practitioners in that setting.

The PIE system requires that every client be described on each of several dimensions called factors. Each factor refers to a different class of information. For a classification system to have maximum usefulness, there must be sufficient data to provide an adequate picture of the client but not so much as to befuddle those who would use the description to plan interventions.

There are four factors in the PIE system. The first two factors constitute the core social work description. The second two factors identify mental and physical health problems using classification systems from other professions. All four factors are needed to provide a comprehensive picture of a client's problems.

The PIE system describes the client's problem complex in the following format:

Factor I   Social Functioning Problems, type, severity, duration, coping ability
Factor II   Environmental Problems, severity, duration
Factor III   Mental Health Problems
Factor IV   Physical health problems

On Factor I the practitioner identifies and codes the client's social role problems. There can be and usually is more than one Factor I problem. The practitioner also identifies and codes each problem's type, the severity of the disruption caused by the problem, the duration of the problem, and the client's coping capacity for dealing with each problem.

On Factor II the practitioner identifies not only the environmental conditions or problems affecting Factor I problems but also the severity of the disruption caused by each problem and each problem's duration. There can also be more than one Factor II problem.

Factors I and II form the core description of a client's social functioning problems and generally are the primary focus of social work intervention.

Factors III and IV describe the client's mental and physical health condition. These may affect social functioning but are not necessarily the direct focus of the social work practitioner, although many social work practitioners are trained and licensed to treat mental disorders. This separation of problems into four factors and the primacy given to social role and environmental problems are intended to emphasize the importance of the client's social functioning—a focus that frequently is difficult to maintain when attention is directed to the usually more vivid Factors III and IV. Thus, the social worker's emphasis is on the social role or environmental problems of a client who may or may not also have a mental or physical disorder. Although the primary focus of PIE is not on the mental and physical problems, interventions may and often do include medical and psychiatric treatment.

Factor III permits the practitioner to indicate any current mental, personality, or developmental disorder or condition that is potentially relevant to the understanding of or intervention with the individual. These conditions are listed on Axes I and II of the *Diagnostic and Statistical Manual of Mental Disorders, Fourth Edition* (DSM-IV) (American Psychiatric Association, 1994). It is assumed that the practitioner will be familiar with the use of DSM-IV or will obtain consultation on assessing mental disorders. Thus, the use of DSM-IV is not discussed in detail in this manual.

Factor IV permits the practitioner to indicate any current physical disorder or condition that is potentially relevant to the understanding or management of the social role or environmental problems of a client. Factor IV is equivalent to Axis III in DSM-IV. These are the conditions exclusive of the mental disorders section of the *International Classification of Diseases–Ninth Revision–Clinical Modification* (ICD-9-CM) (U.S. Department of Health and Human Services, 1991).

The social worker should inquire routinely about any significant physical problems and record the results of this inquiry on Factor IV. As a professional who is not licensed to make physical diagnoses, the social worker should note the source of the information. For example, the worker might record the results of an intake evaluation and note on Factor IV "Diabetes (by report of the client)," or "Asthma (diagnosed by Dr. X)," or "Client reports no physical problems."

In some instances, a client's physical condition may be an important source of social role or environmental problems (for example, acquired immune deficiency syndrome [AIDS] in a client with a Lover Role Problem, loss type). In another instance the physical disorder may not be the source of the client's problems, but it may be important in planning an overall intervention strategy (for example, genital herpes in a person with a Spouse Role Problem, ambivalence type). In yet another instance, the practitioner may wish to note significant associated physical findings (for example, history of heart attacks in a client with a Worker Role Problem, loss type). The practitioner should refer to ICD-9-CM for further information pertaining to coding on this factor. If ICD-9-CM is unavailable, the practitioner may describe the physical disorder in lay language (for example, severe asthma as reported by client).

References

American Psychiatric Association. (1994). *Diagnostic and statistical manual of mental disorders* (4th ed.). Washington, DC: American Psychiatric Press.

U.S. Department of Health and Human Services. (1991). *International classification of Diseases–9th revision–clinical modification* (4th ed.). Washington, DC: U.S. Government Printing Office.

2.

Use of the Manual

To use the PIE system effectively, the practitioner should become familiar with the problem groups in both Factors I and II. Factor I consists of four social role groups and nine common interactional problem types. The manual first describes and illustrates social role problems and types, and then it describes the conceptualization of environment used in the PIE system. Six groups are used to describe problems in the environment. Instruction is then provided on the use of the Severity, Duration, and Coping Indexes used to amplify descriptions on Factors I and II.

In addition to the written descriptions, each section provides numerical codes to record client problem situations in a uniform, capsulated manner. The use of the coding system is not required but may be particularly helpful for administrators and researchers who want a snapshot of the kinds of problems presented by an agency's clientele or in a particular community.

After a careful reading and study of this manual, most social workers should be able to describe their clients' social role and environmental problems using PIE. Some general guidelines will facilitate this process.

General Guidelines

- There need not be a problem on each factor.
- If a problem is stated, it should be possible to document it.
- The problem description can be done at various points in the social worker–client interaction (intake, beginning, midpoint, or termination), and the description may change over time.
- The social worker may record as many problems as have been identified on each factor, but because one of the goals of this coding system is to clarify the focus for social work intervention, he or she should emphasize problems that have a significant impact on a client's social functioning. Rarely will a practitioner need to record more than four problems.
- The recording of a problem should be in terms of the social worker's assessment. That is, the social worker should record what he or she perceives as a problem, even if the client may not necessarily agree with the assessment at the time it is done.
- In its present form, this manual is to be used only for coding the social functioning problems of adults. An adult is a person 18 years or older or a legally emancipated minor.
- The use of the coding system is secondary to using the problem descriptions. Practitioners should first master the problem description before using the coding system.

Factor I: Social Role Problem Identification

The practitioner should record on Factor I all the client's problems in social role functioning identified at the time of the assessment. To provide a comprehensive description, the following seven steps should be followed:

1. Identify all of the social roles with which the client is having difficulty. If there is more than one problem, indicate the primary or presenting problem. For example, a client with a problem in his marriage would be noted as having a Spouse Role Problem (primary problem).

2. Identify the types for each problem. For example, if the problem in a marriage is the desertion of a spouse, the type of problem would be identified as loss.

3. Locate the appropriate social role and type codes. An explanation of the coding system will be presented later. The coding for a Spouse Role Problem, loss type is 1 2 5 0.XXX.

4. Determine and code the severity rating. For example, if the Spouse Role Problem, loss type is determined to be high in severity, it would be coded as 4, Spouse Role Problem, loss type, high severity, 1250.4XX.

5. Determine and code the duration rating. For example, if the Spouse Role Problem had been going on for three years, it would be coded as 2, Spouse Role Problem, loss type, high severity, 1250.42X.

6. Determine and code the coping rating. For example, if the client had a history of successfully coping with difficult situations, the coping rating would be 3, Spouse Role Problem, loss type, high severity, one to five years duration, adequate coping skills, 1250.423.

7. Repeat this process for each additional social role problem identified on Factor I.

Factor II: Environmental Problem Identification

On Factor II the social worker should record environmental problems—problems in the social institutions in the client's community that affect the client's social role functioning. To provide a comprehensive description, the social worker should follow these six steps:

1. Identify the general social system that is affecting the client's social role problem. For example, a client with a Spouse Role Problem, loss type, high severity, one to five years duration, adequate coping skills, is also experiencing stress because of a high level of violence in his neighborhood. This problem lies within the Health, Safety, and Social Services System, 8XXX.XX.

2. Identify the subcategory within the social system under which the environmental problem exists. This Health Safety, and Social Services System problem lies within the safety subcategory, 82XX.XX.

3. Under the appropriate subcategory, identify the specific environmental problem. Within the safety subcategory, there is a specific problem called violence or crime in neighborhood, which is coded as 8201. Thus,

Health, Safety, and Social Services System, safety, violence or crime in neighborhood, is coded as 8201.XX.

4. Determine and code the severity of the problem. If the safety problem is very high in severity, this is coded as 5. Thus, the coding would be Health Safety, and Social Services System, safety, violence or crime in neighborhood, very high severity, 8201.5X.

5. Determine and code the duration of the problem. If the safety problem has been going on for five months, this is coded as 4. Thus, the coding would be Health, Safety, and Social Services, safety, violence or crime in neighborhood, very high severity, one to six months duration, 8201.54.

6. Repeat this process for each additional environmental problem identified on Factor II.

Factor III: Mental Health Problem Identification

The social worker should record on Factor III any current mental disorder or condition that is potentially relevant to understanding the client's problem. Such conditions are listed on Axes I and II of DSM-IV. Because DSM-IV codes are not listed in this manual, the social worker should refer to DSM-IV for a discussion of their use. Axes I and II diagnoses and codes are recorded under Factor III, using the terminology and codes in DSM-IV.

Factor IV: Physical Health Problem Identification

The social worker should record on Factor IV any current physical disorder or condition that is potentially relevant to understanding or managing the client's problems. Ideally, the social worker should use the terminology and coding contained in the ICD-9-CM. Because this manual does not include ICD-9-CM codes, the social worker should refer to ICD-9-CM for additional information pertaining to coding on this factor. If ICD-9-CM is unavailable, the practitioner may describe the physical disorder in lay language. The social worker should note the source of the information pertaining to a physical disorder or condition. For example, "By client report," or "By Dr. X's report."

Other Considerations

When the social worker identifies more than one problem on a factor, then the problem identified as chiefly responsible for the request for service should be designated as the primary problem. The primary problem can be designated as in either Factor I or Factor II. If, in the social worker's judgment, the presenting problem is not the primary problem, the worker should distinguish between the two problems. For example, if a person with an ongoing Parent Role Problem comes for treatment of a Spouse Role Problem, the description should be listed as such:

Factor I   1250.XXX   Spouse Role Problem, loss type (presenting problem)

1110.XXX   Parent Role Problem, power type (primary problem)

In some instances, enough information will be available to provide a role problem listing, but the practitioner may wish to indicate a significant degree of uncertainty by writing "provisional" following the description.

Factor I   1110.XXX   Parent Role Problem, power type (provisional, rule out Spouse Role Problem, ambivalence type)

Sometimes an assessment or evaluation yields insufficient information to make a specific problem listing, and the practitioner may wish to defer making a listing. This may be indicated on Factor I or II in the following way:

Factor I   9999.999   Problem listing deferred
Factor II   9999.99   Problem listing deferred

If there is no problem on a factor, the coding is

Factor I   0000.000   No problem
Factor II   0000.00   No problem

3.

Factor I: Social Role Functioning

Most clients of social workers present themselves or are referred for help because they are having difficulties in their social role functioning, such as in their relationships with others in their family, at work or at school, or in the community. Social functioning is a person's overall performance in his or her social roles. A primary goal of any social work intervention is to optimize the client's social functioning.

A person's social role can be defined in terms of fulfilling a recognized and regulated position in society such as a parent, student, or employee. Tradition, law, and societal and family values define the content of roles. Although the major functions of the role remain generally the same across cultures, the way in which the functions are accomplished may vary from culture to culture and from subgroup to subgroup within a specific culture.

Social Role Descriptions and Codes

Described below are the social role problems used in the PIE system and their codes. Social roles are grouped into four major categories: Family Roles, Other Interpersonal Roles, Occupational Roles, and Special Life Situation Roles. The descriptions of social role problems below include illustrative examples to clarify the concepts. These examples should encompass most social role problems that are likely to be encountered in social work practice. Whenever possible, the practitioner should use a specific social role code rather than the "Other" code.

Social Role Problem	Codes
Family Roles	1000.XXX
Parent Role	1100.XXX
Spouse Role	1200.XXX
Child Role	1300.XXX
Sibling Role	1400.XXX
Other Family Role	1500.XXX
Significant Other Role	1600.XXX
Other Interpersonal Roles	2000.XXX
Lover Role	2100.XXX
Friend Role	2200.XXX
Neighbor Role	2300.XXX
Member Role	2400.XXX
Other Interpersonal Role	2500.XXX

Occupational Roles	3000.XXX
Worker Role–Paid Economy	3100.XXX
Worker Role–Home	3200.XXX
Worker Role–Volunteer	3300.XXX
Student Role	3400.XXX
Other Occupational Role	3500.XXX
Special Life Situation Roles	4000.XXX
Consumer Role	4100.XXX
Inpatient/Client Role	4200.XXX
Outpatient/Client Role	4300.XXX
Probationer/Parolee Role	4400.XXX
Prisoner Role	4500.XXX
Immigrant Role–Legal	4600.XXX
Immigrant Role–Undocumented	4700.XXX
Immigrant Role–Refugee	4800.XXX
Other Special Life Situation Roles	4900.XXX

On Factor I each social role problem is designated by a four-digit number. For example, a Parent Role Problem is 11XX.XXX and a Spouse Role Problem is 12XX.XXX. Each type of role problem is incorporated into the social role number in the last two digits; for example, the power type is XX10.XXX and the ambivalence type is XX20.XXX. Thus, a social role problem can be written and numerically coded by combining the social role code and the type of role problem code, for example, Parent Role Problem, power type, 1110.XXX.

The first digit to the right of the decimal point (_____.X__) designates the severity of the problem, the second digit (_____._X_) designates the duration of the problem, and the third digit (_____.__X) designates the coping ability of the client. The Severity, Duration, and Coping Indexes are discussed in another section of this manual.

Definitions of Social Roles

1000.XXX: Family Roles

Family roles are social roles that are played out in the context of a family setting in which the individuals are linked by blood, law, or informal arrangements.

1100.XXX: Parent Role. Biology and society have delegated to the parent the major responsibilities for nurturing and socializing each successive generation. At a minimum, these responsibilities include assisting with developmental tasks, providing physical protection, transmitting family and cultural lore, and providing a family and cultural identity.

A person assuming Parent Role responsibility may be a natural parent, stepparent, adoptive parent, or someone legally or informally assuming the responsibilities for a specific minor. Who exercises the Parent Role and how he or she fulfills its responsibilities may vary from family to family and from culture to culture. In most societies, the parent has legal responsibility for the welfare of the child, and cultural expectations of minimal parenting requirements are prescribed by law.

The following are examples of Parent Role Problems:

- A single mother who feels that she is unable to control her children
- A father who loses contact with his children after a divorce
- A foster parent who is distressed when a child is removed from his or her care.

1200.XXX: Spouse Role. The Spouse Role encompasses the responsibilities and expectations assigned to each of two persons who have formed a legal, religious, or private union for the purposes of basic physical and economic security, emotional and sexual gratification, social recognition, companionship, and in some instances, procreation.

The following are examples of Spouse Role Problems:

- A person who is depressed after a divorce
- A woman who is distressed that her live-in female lover is unwilling to be monogamous
- A man who is physically abusive to his wife.

1300.XXX: Child Role. Because this manual is limited to the classification of the social role problems of adults, the Child Role code is limited to adults who present a problem in their relationship with their parents.

The Child Role consists of the performance of a series of physical, emotional, and intellectual tasks of increasing complexity and differentiation. Performing the Child Role prepares one for assuming the responsibilities, expectations, and privileges of other societal roles. A major responsibility of the Child Role involves receiving and then either preserving or changing family and societal customs and identity. A person most often performs the Child Role in relationship to another person who is performing the Parent Role. However, performance of the Child Role is not dependent on the presence of parents, nor is it confined to any one period of the life cycle.

The following are examples of Child Role Problems:

- A 35-year-old woman who thinks that her parents treat her like a child whenever she visits them
- A 63-year-old women who is overwhelmed with the care of her aging mother
- A 28-year-old man who remains fearful of his stepfather, who molested him when he was five years old.

1400.XXX: Sibling Role. Because the PIE system is limited to the classification of the social role problems of adults, Sibling Role problems are limited to adults who present a problem in relation to brothers and sisters.

The sharing of family history, ethnic or cultural identity, intrafamily responsibilities, and expectations of the natural, adoptive, step-, or surrogate offspring of common parents is the major element of the Sibling Role. Siblings may share one or more common parents or stepparents. In many cultures sex and birth order determine the specific performance requirements in the Sibling Role.

The following are examples of Sibling Role Problems:

- A person who is experiencing a conflict with his siblings over the division of their parents' estate
- A 49-year-old woman who is fighting with her 53-year-old brother about his excessive drinking
- A 29-year-old woman who feels ignored when her long-lost 35-year-old stepbrother reappears on the scene.

1500.XXX: Other Family Roles. The Other Family Role is reserved for someone who, by blood ties or by formal or informal agreement, serves in the role of aunt, uncle, grandparent, cousin, or in-law. This role also would include spouses, grandparents, and other relatives from previous marriages. Other Family Roles are usually less defined in American society than the family roles described above. People occupying these roles who are older than a client often perform, to a lesser or greater extent, some of the responsibilities of the Parent Role, whereas those closer in age to the client often perform some of the responsibilities of the Sibling or Friend Role. The type of Other Family Role should be specified in the listing.

The following are examples of Other Family Role Problems:

- A woman who dislikes the woman her son has married (mother-in-law role)
- A grandmother who loses contact with her grandchildren after a divorce (grandmother role)
- A long-term family friend who is treated as an uncle by the family, but is then snubbed by other members of the family because he is not related by blood (uncle role).

1600.XXX: Significant Other Role. The Significant Other Role is reserved for a person who is accepted as a member of the nuclear or extended family. This person affects the functioning of that family by assuming, augmenting, supporting, or influencing the performance of one or more of the other family roles. This person does not fall into any of the Other Family Role categories.

The following are examples of Significant Other Role Problems:

- A family friend who is distressed because for the first time in 20 years she is not invited to a family-only birthday party
- A long-term roommate of a man who is distressed because the man wants him to move out
- A family friend who is called in to take care of the children in a single-parent family when the mother gets drunk each week.

2000.XXX: Other Interpersonal Roles

Other interpersonal roles are social roles that are played out in interpersonal relationships between individuals who are not members of the same family, but who, because of physical proximity or common interests, interact with each other.

2100.XXX: Lover Role. The Lover Role denotes an intimate sexual, or potentially sexual, relationship between individuals of the same or the opposite sex. It includes the behaviors of dating and courting, but it excludes living together and having a commitment to a long-term relationship. Lovers who live together and are committed to a long-term relationship would be placed into the Spouse Role.

The following are examples of Lover Role Problems:

- A woman who is questioning whether she should live with her boyfriend
- A gay man who is tired of fighting with his lover about having to hide their relationship
- A woman who feels that she is constantly getting into love relationships with "losers."

2200.XXX: Friend Role. In the Friend Role a person maintains a relationship with another person of the same or opposite sex for the purpose of mutual emotional and spiritual support and companionship. The role usually does not include a sexual relationship because this would be included in the Lover Role.

The following are examples of Friend Role Problems:

- A woman who is upset that her best friend is ignoring her since she got involved with a lover
- A man who is wondering how to be supportive of his friend who is undergoing a difficult custody battle
- A woman who is having a fight with a friend who has not returned money lent to her.

2300.XXX: Neighbor Role. The Neighbor Role is primarily a function of geographic proximity resulting in occasional contact between people, usually less frequently than between friends. The basic responsibility of the role is to preserve the health and safety of the shared living environment. Neighbors may also serve as a source of support in a crisis.

The following are examples of Neighbor Role Problems:

- A man who is concerned that his neighbor is selling drugs out of his house
- A woman who feels isolated in her new neighborhood because she does not know anyone
- A person who is concerned about the trend in the neighborhood to tear down older homes to construct apartment buildings.

2400.XXX: Member Role. Voluntary affiliation and participation with a group of individuals associated for a common purpose and adhering to mutually agreed-upon beliefs or regulations are the primary characteristics of the Member Role. The specific responsibilities and expectations of the role vary according to the purpose and structure of the group, which can be organized for political, religious, social, recreational, professional, or other reasons.

The following are examples of Member Role Problems:

- A person who is uncertain whether to run for office in a professional association

- A person who is distressed by the internal conflict in an environmental action group
- A woman who is concerned that she may be asked to leave her church group when it is discovered that she has been embezzling funds.

2500.XXX: Other Interpersonal Role. The social worker should use Other Interpersonal Role to describe an interpersonal role problem that does not involve Family, Occupational, or Special Life Situation Roles and does not fall into the other categories in this section. In the listing, the social worker should specify the type of interpersonal role.

The following are examples of Other Interpersonal Role Problems:

- An amateur baseball player who is always arguing with the umpire (athlete role)
- A man who is upset because he has to undergo an audit by the Internal Revenue Service (citizen role)
- A woman who is depressed because of the death of her cat (pet owner role).

3000.XXX: Occupational Roles

Occupational roles are social roles that are performed in the paid or unpaid economy or in academic institutions.

3100.XXX: Worker Role–Paid Economy. The Worker Role–Paid Economy includes all responsibilities and expectations associated with the activities that a person performs to acquire the economic resources needed to provide for food, clothing, shelter, transportation, recreation, health, and personal care. This role involves work of a paid nature outside of or at the home. The specifics of the role vary, depending on the nature and status of the activity. Unemployed and retired people may be included in this role designation if the situation causing discomfort is associated with the loss of or change in the worker role.

The following are examples of Worker Role–Paid Economy Problems:

- A man who is distressed about his impending retirement
- A woman who feels that she is treated unfairly by her boss
- A woman who is worried that she will not be able to handle a promotion.

3200.XXX: Worker Role–Home. The Worker Role–Home includes all responsibilities and expectations associated with the activities a person performs to maintain a home—such as shopping, cooking, cleaning, and sewing—but does not include parenting. The role involves unpaid work performed in the home by a person of either sex. A person who is paid for such work would fit into the Worker Role–Paid Economy category.

The following are examples of Worker Role–Home Problems:

- A woman who is angry that her roommates do not clean up after themselves
- A woman who feels that her husband is unwilling to assist her in doing the housework
- A man who experiences ridicule from his family because he wants to stay home and do housework and let his wife support the family.

3300.XXX: Worker Role–Volunteer. The Worker Role–Volunteer assumes some of the responsibilities of the paid worker but is not paid for this work. This role often is performed in health care, community agencies, education, and religious settings, but does not include work performed in professional associations, which would be included under the Member Role.

The following are examples of Worker Role–Volunteer Problems:

- A resident of a psychiatric halfway house who is having trouble performing a volunteer job
- A volunteer in a children's agency who is overly involved with the agency's clients and is sabotaging the staff's case plans
- A hospital volunteer who is distressed about the deaths of many of his or her patients.

3400.XXX: Student Role. The primary function of the Student Role is acquiring and assimilating knowledge and skills. The nature and complexity of the material the person studies and the method of acquisition help determine the responsibilities and expectations of the role. A person can assume the Student Role at any age.

The following are examples of Student Role Problems:

- A college student who fails all of his classes
- A woman who has been accepted to medical school but is unsure if she can handle the workload
- A 65-year-old woman who feels out of place returning to the university to complete her education.

3500.XXX: Other Occupational Role. The social worker should use Other Occupational Role to denote occupational role problems that do not fit into the above roles or that have characteristics of two subcategories but do not fit into one. In the listing, the worker should specify the type of Other Occupational Role.

The following are examples of Other Occupational Role Problems:

- An Olympic athlete who performs poorly and misses the chance to win a medal in her sport and turn professional (Amateur Athlete/Worker Role–Paid Economy)
- A social work student in an agency who is upset because her small stipend has been canceled (Student Role/Volunteer Role)
- A student in a training program who is placed in the same work setting where he is a paid worker and has difficulties dealing with the sometimes conflictual demands of being both a trainee and a regular staff person (Student Role/Worker Role–Paid Economy).

4000.XXX: Special Life-Situation Roles

Throughout the course of their lives, people may voluntarily or involuntarily assume time-limited, situation-specific roles in addition to or in place of other possible roles. Most frequently, societal, legal, institutional, and professional expectations govern the responsibilities and expectations of these roles.

4100.XXX: Consumer Role. The Consumer Role is assumed by someone who contracts to receive services or goods from a provider. These providers can include attorneys, real estate agents, or other business persons. Excluded from this category are providers of services to treat mental, physical, or psychosocial disorders. These are included under the Patient/Client Roles. The Consumer Role involves voluntary and active participation on the part of the person who seeks services or goods and who is free to initiate or terminate the contract. This role usually includes the exchange of money for goods and services.

The following are examples of Consumer Role Problems:

- A man who is dissatisfied with how his mechanic has repaired his car
- A woman who believes that her real estate agent lied to her by not telling her about major defects in her house
- A man who thinks that his attorney is running up his bill by spending more time than is necessary on his case.

4200.XXX: Inpatient/Client Role. The Inpatient/Client Role is assumed by a person who is defined by helping professionals as using or needing help in an institutional setting, such as in a psychiatric hospital, general hospital, or nursing home. The person may or may not recognize the need for help.

The following are examples of Inpatient/Client Role Problems:

- A long-term resident of a psychiatric hospital who is unable to adjust to life on a new unit
- An elderly woman who becomes assaultive when the staff at her nursing home are inattentive to her needs
- A seriously ill patient who wishes to leave the hospital against medical advice.

4300.XXX: Outpatient/Client Role. The Outpatient/Client Role is similar to the Inpatient/Client Role because it is assumed by a person who is defined by helping professionals as using or being in need of help except that help is received outside of an institutional setting. The person may or may not recognize the need for help.

The following are examples of Outpatient/Client Role Problems:

- A woman who feels that her physician prescribes tranquilizers instead of taking the time to assess her problem
- A seriously suicidal man who disagrees with his therapist's recommendation that he be referred for antidepressant medication
- A woman who is in love with her podiatrist.

4400.XXX: Probationer/Parolee Role. The Probationer/Parolee Role is assumed by a person who has been convicted of or pled guilty to a criminal charge and who is monitored or supervised by officers of the criminal justice system in lieu of or after serving a sentence.

The following are examples of Probationer/Parolee Role Problems:

- A man who is having trouble living up to the conditions of his probation
- A parolee who cannot return to his hometown because of community outcry about the nature of his crime

- A woman who feels that her parole officer does not like her.

4500.XXX: Prisoner Role. The Prisoner Role is assumed by a person who is incarcerated. The prisoner may be awaiting trial or may have been sentenced for an infraction of the law.

    The following are examples of Prisoner Role Problems:

- A man convicted of child molestation who is worried about being treated harshly by other prisoners
- A man jailed for traffic violations who suffers a psychotic break
- A woman who is worried about a new guard transferred to her unit who has a reputation for being cruel.

4600.XXX: Immigrant Role–Legal. The Immigrant Role–Legal is assumed by a person who has legally moved from one country to another. The immigrant may have to deal with the loss of an old way of life, language difficulties, learning new values, hostile reactions from the citizens of the new country, or culture conflict.

    The following are examples of Immigrant Role–Legal Problems:

- A man raised in France by French parents who were raised in the United States. The man is not sure where he fits in when he immigrates to the United States
- A Brazilian woman who is hindered by her difficulties in learning English
- A woman from Hong Kong who is worried she will lose her traditional values in the United States.

4700.XXX: Immigrant Role–Undocumented. The Immigrant Role–Undocumented is similar to the Immigrant Role–Legal except that the undocumented immigrant did not immigrate legally and may have to deal with his or her fear of apprehension by the authorities.

    The following are examples of Immigrant Role–Undocumented Problems:

- A man from Haiti who is worried that he will not qualify for amnesty under a government program
- A Canadian who pretends to be from the United States and fears she will be found out and reported to the immigration authorities
- A Mexican man who has been caught by the immigration authorities for the fifth time in a year and is being returned to Mexico.

4800.XXX: Immigrant Role–Refugee. The Immigrant Role–Refugee is similar to the Immigrant Role–Legal except that the refugee is in flight from his or her native land because of political or religious persecution.

    The following are examples of Immigrant Role–Refugee Problems:

- A Cuban living in the United States who is afraid she will never see her family again
- A Chinese dissident who is afraid of being killed if he returns to China
- A Central American refugee who is worried about being gunned down by Central American death squads operating in the United States.

4900.XXX: Other Special Life-Situation Role. The social worker should use Other Special Life-Situation Role to denote other roles that are not included above. These are usually time-limited and situation-specific roles that people may experience at different times in their lives. The specific Other Special Life-Situation Role should be noted in the listing.

Types of Role Problems

After a social role problem has been identified, it is necessary to describe its major dynamics that might help decide what intervention might be useful. For example, a client with a Spouse Role Problem who is in conflict with a spouse is significantly different from a client with a Spouse Role Problem resulting from the spouse's death. A client with a Worker Role–Paid Economy Problem who is in conflict with an employer is significantly different from a client with a Worker Role–Paid Economy Problem who is being transferred to a less prestigious assignment.

The term "types" is used in the PIE system to describe the kind of interactional difficulty that is occurring or has occurred between the client and another person. It is assumed that a relationship is now strained, disrupted, or broken. It is the social worker's task to describe the nature of the strain, disruption, or break, both to provide a clearer picture of the problem and to facilitate remedial interventions.

The following list of problem types attempts to provide standardized terminology for describing the most commonly observed characteristics of frequently occurring social functioning problems. It is important to keep in mind that both the social role functioning problem and the type are descriptive of the client's difficulty and not of the other person in the relationship. In most interactional difficulties, forces from both persons are involved, so it is important when typing the problem to focus on the client presenting the problem. Thus, an abused spouse's problem might be typed as victimization, whereas the abusing spouse's problem might be typed as power.

After identifying the social role area in which the client's problem exists, the social worker chooses the particular type that is most descriptive of the interactional dynamics presented by the client. The list of the problem types includes illustrative case examples to clarify the concepts. These problem types are believed to be descriptive of most situations that are likely to be encountered in social work practice. Because the types are not mutually exclusive, it is possible that a client's type of role problem may include more than one descriptor. If this occurs, it is advisable to identify the dominant type, or if more than one type is prominent, to use the mixed-type category.

Type	Codes
Power type	XX10.XXX
Ambivalence type	XX20.XXX
Responsibility type	XX30.XXX
Dependency type	XX40.XXX
Loss type	XX50.XXX
Isolation type	XX60.XXX
Victimization type	XX70.XXX
Mixed type	XX80.XXX
Other type	XX90.XXX

XX10.XXX: Power Type

Problems of the power type generally involve the misuse or abuse of physical or psychological power. Power is the ability to do, act, perform, or produce. Power also includes the ability to influence others. Power is the biopsychosocial force a person possesses and is able to express. Related to power type problems are problems involving conflict. Conflict is a sharp disagreement or the opposition of ideas, interests, or other elements between people. Conflict is a normal phenomenon that is inherent in and is generated by role performance. The tensions generated by conflict have the potential of motivating the persons involved toward problem solving and resolution. However, these tensions can, and frequently do, have maladaptive consequences. Power and conflict problems can run the gamut from mild disagreement, to abuse, to murder, and to open warfare.

Case Example. The rebellious behavior of a Marine officer's adolescent daughter is a personal threat to his authority in his Parent Role. Accustomed to having his orders obeyed, the officer responds to his child's actions with arbitrary threats, which intensify the rebellion and escalate the interpersonal distress. When it comes to carrying out the threats, the officer finds that neither his wife nor the law will allow him to do so. His anger and frustration result in inappropriate and maladaptive behavior (child abuse). Thus, this individual's difficulties in his role of parent could be expressed as 1110.XXX, Parent Role Problem, power type.

The following are examples of other power problems:

- A husband who refuses to let his wife work outside the home (1210.XXX, Spouse Role)
- An authoritarian boss who must know everything about his employees' personal lives (3110.XXX, Worker Role–Paid Economy)
- A man who strikes a mechanic because he is dissatisfied with the repair work on his car (4110.XXX, Consumer Role).

XX20.XXX: Ambivalence Type

Ambivalence is a state of internal tension involving conflicting feelings about a person or thing. It is a common occurrence that is inherent in and is generated by role performance expectations. The tensions generated by ambivalence have the potential of motivating the people involved toward problem solving and resolution. A person's ambivalence may also result in role performance behavior that confuses or provokes others.

Case Example. A 26-year-old woman is feeling conflicted about continuing with the therapist she has seen for nine months. She often dreads going to sessions because she knows that painful material will come up. At the end of the session she is usually pleased that she kept her appointment. The next day, however, she finds herself full of dread again about seeing her therapist. She contemplates leaving a message on her therapist's answering machine telling her that she has decided not to see her anymore. This cycle repeats itself week after week. Thus, this client's problem could be expressed as 4320.XXX, Outpatient/Client Role Problem, ambivalence type.

The following are other examples of ambivalence problems:

- A college student who can't decide between majoring in art—his true love—or business—which is more likely to allow him to make a living (3420.XXX, Student Role)
- A woman who is ambivalent about staying in a relationship (2120.XXX, Lover Role)
- A prisoner who gets into gang fights despite his negative feelings about gangs (4520.XXX, Prisoner Role).

XX30.XXX: Responsibility Type

Responsibility is the obligation to fulfill certain role requirements. A performance expectation is what a person, the person's significant others, and his or her community define as the adequate fulfillment of these requirements.

Role performance expectations, prescribed behavior, assigned responsibilities, and sanctions for inadequate performance are defined by a person's community, transmitted through that community's culture, and internalized by the person. If these responsibilities are felt to be overwhelming, oppressive, or too difficult, the person may be unhappy or distressed. The person's sense of well-being depends on seeing himself or herself as having fulfilled role expectations. A negative self-evaluation with respect to role performance may have serious effects on self-esteem.

Case Example. A highly productive, extremely industrious insurance broker now finds himself unable to produce as before. Not only does he berate himself for his lack of motivation, but he finds that his business partner and long-standing friend rather quickly moves from being supportive to being angry, threatening to dissolve the partnership if things do not improve. This combination of internal and external stresses leads the broker to a state of despair and hopelessness. Thus, this man's problem could be coded as 3130.XXX, Worker Role–Paid Economy Problem, responsibility type.

The following are other examples of responsibility problems:

- A woman who feels unable to meet the responsibilities of being a full-time mother (1130.XXX, Parent Role)
- A new officer in a community organization who feels overwhelmed by her responsibilities (2430.XXX, Member Role)
- A landlord who is unable to maintain his building and has received a notice from the health department (3530.XXX, Other Occupational Role, Landlord).

XX40.XXX: Dependency Type

Dependency is the condition of being influenced, controlled, or supported by another person. Dependency needs exist in almost every person. They are normal elements of the human condition that vary situationally and with the life cycle. Cultural patterns have a strong influence in determining how dependency needs are met. If a person's dependency needs are not adequately met, the individual's role performance may be negatively affected.

A correlate of dependence is independence. Independence is freedom from the influence, control, or manipulation of others. It is the ability of a person to assume responsibility in directing his or her life. To be independent is to initiate behavior based on one's inner convictions and resources without being unduly influenced by others.

Strivings for independence, mastery, and self-actualization are drives that characterize human growth and development. Most people have the wish to attain competence in the performance of social roles. Perceived or real obstacles to achieving independence may produce frustration, anger, rebellion, and dysfunctional role performance behavior. Chronic frustration of these strivings usually leads to depression and abdication of both responsibility and hope. Cultural patterns set role performance expectations with respect to independent behavior. Failure to live up to these expectations, whether perceived or real, may lead to problems in social functioning.

Case Example. A 22-year-old college junior is involved in a struggle to determine his own identity. He has remained in school at the insistence of his father, who is paying for his education. He has changed majors several times, but he still does not know what he wants to do. His family has not been receptive to his attempts to discuss this problem. He has turned to his girlfriend for advice, but has found her to be frightened by his lack of decisiveness. Although this client is experiencing both Student and Friend Role Problems, his primary problem could be coded as 1340.XXX, Child Role Problem, dependency type.

The following are other examples of dependency problems:

- A man without a family of his own who spends most of his time with a friend's family is distressed that they now ask him not to spend so much time with them (1640.XXX, Significant Other Role)
- A woman who is unable to go out of her house without the assistance of her best friend (2240.XXX, Friend Role)
- A seriously ill woman who defers all decisions about her health care to her physician and her husband (4340.XXX, Outpatient/Client Role).

XX50.XXX: Loss Type

Separation is the breaking apart from a person or thing to which a person has attached emotional significance. Loss is a permanent separation with a grieving process that usually accompanies such an event. The loss or threatened loss of a significant person by separation, death, or physical distance can create anxiety, resentment, anger, hopelessness, and a lack of energy, will, or ability to deal with the change. Social role performance under these circumstances becomes difficult.

For many people the loss of a role is in itself a highly significant life event. A change in status is also frequently experienced as a loss and is included under this type. Status is a person's condition or position with regard to the law, a relationship, a group, the community, or society as a whole. Status generally reflects a stable arrangement over a period of time. A change in status usually disrupts this stability and may create distress.

Both real status and perceived status are aspects of social role performance. A person who is unsure of his or her status in a particular social situation or relationship, or a person who is unhappy with his or her status, may develop social functioning problems. A person moving into a new role that involves status change may feel anxious and distressed. The life cycle, life events, and physical impairment characteristically bring about status changes that require adjustment and lifestyle reorganization, often causing a disruption of existing social roles and a need for accommodation to new and sometimes unwanted roles.

Case Example. A 60-year-old business executive has achieved the recognition of his family and peers for his accomplishments. He recently suffered a marked decline in his cognitive functioning, apparently as a result of a slight stroke. His employer has transferred him to a less demanding post. He has become quite depressed and obsessively preoccupied with worries about the future. This man's role problem may be coded as 3150.XXX, Worker Role–Paid Economy, loss type.

The following are other examples of loss problems:

- An undocumented immigrant who has been a successful business executive but who is apprehended and placed in detention (4750.XXX, Immigrant Role–Undocumented)
- A man whose wife dies in an accident (1250.XXX, Spouse Role)
- A client whose therapist moves away (4350.XXX, Outpatient/Client Role).

XX60.XXX: Isolation Type

To be isolated is to be apart from others, to be alone. Withdrawal is the process by which an individual can isolate himself or herself, usually in response to a perceived hurt or other stress.

Individuals who are shy, fearful, or uncomfortable in their relationships and prescribed social roles may tend to isolate themselves from what they perceive as the stresses of participation. For some, this is a chronic state related to long-standing problems of self-esteem or a mental disorder. For others, it is a situational response. The loss of, or hurt in, an important relationship may lead to withdrawal from this relationship and possibly others. People in new situations or communities may have problems establishing new relationships, and the social roles familiar to them may not be adaptive.

Case Example. A 38-year-old single woman has always been very shy. Although she desires friendships, she continues to isolate herself from others, fearful of how they would respond if they really knew her. This woman's Friend Role problem could be coded as 2260.XXX, Friend Role Problem, isolation type.

The following are other examples of isolation problems:

- A man in a nursing home who no longer communicates with the other patients (4260.XXX, Inpatient/Client Role)
- A young man who has been unsuccessful in dating withdraws from all social contacts (2260.XXX, Friend Role)

- A Vietnam veteran who moves to a cabin in the woods because he can no longer tolerate living around other people (4960.XXX, Other Special Life-Situation Role, Veteran).

XX70.XXX: Victimization Type

Intimidation is the fear of anticipated harm. Victimization is turning this fear into a behavioral pattern in which a person gives in to fears, giving up his or her power to deal with the intimidator or victimizer.

Relationships that result in a person feeling intimidated or victimized may bring about serious role functioning problems. Drastic changes in a person's social or occupational performance may cause the individual to feel powerless, alienated, personally deficient, and without the ability to control or influence the situation. Perceived threats, whether real or not, can be very stressful, leading to feelings of helplessness and anticipation of further harm.

Case Example. A 35-year-old nurse has had a secure job at a county hospital for eight years and was planning to make her career within the system. For the past four years there have been serious funding cutbacks, which have directly affected the resources available to do her job; and this has increased her frustration with the level of patient care that is possible. Her supervisor has not been supportive, telling her that she will just have to make do. When she last complained, her supervisor told her that she would be fired if she complained anymore. Because she cannot afford to lose her job, the nurse has resigned herself to doing what she can and has abdicated her feeling of personal responsibility for the outcome. This woman's role problem may be coded as 3170.XX, Worker Role–Paid Economy, victimization type.

The following are other examples of victimization-type problems:

- A woman who defers to her husband because she fears beatings (1270.XXX, Spouse Role)
- A member of a religious group who has been threatened with excommunication if she speaks out against the group's financial mismanagement (2470.XXX, Member Role)
- An undocumented immigrant who tolerates terrible working conditions (4770.XXX, Immigrant Role–Undocumented).

XX80.XXX: Mixed Type

The social worker should use mixed type when no one dimension of role performance is predominant and when the role problem can best be described by a mixture of dimensions.

Case Example. Because of budget cuts, a woman who has been hospitalized in a state mental hospital ward for the past 10 years is suddenly released. For 10 years she has been taken care of by the hospital staff, and she has lost her ability to take care of herself. She has developed an identity as a chronic schizophrenic who must spend the rest of her life institutionalized. This woman's role problem would be coded as 4280.XXX, Inpatient/Client Role Problem, mixed type (loss type and dependency type).

The following are other examples of mixed-type problems:

- A parent who loses a child and withdraws from the other children (1180.XXX, Parent Role, loss type and isolation type)
- A husband who beats up his wife, on whom he has been very dependent, when he finds out she has been having an affair (1280.XXX, Spouse Role, power type and dependency type)
- A student who is ambivalent about graduating withdraws from her studies and her friends (3480.XXX, Student Role, ambivalence type and isolation type).

XX90.XXX: Other Type

The social worker should use other type when none of the above dimensions of role performance adequately describe the given case situation. The social worker should specify the type in the listing.

4.

Factor II: Person in Environment/Problems in the Environment

In social work a person and his or her environment are regarded as interacting, each influencing and shaping the other. In the social role problems previously listed, attention has been given to interpersonal transactions that affect social functioning. The environmental problems that follow are the factors outside of the client that affect social functioning and well-being. The environment is seen as both the physical and social context in which a person lives. It is the sum total of the natural setting and the human-made circumstances outside of the person. The environment provides both resources and opportunities; it activates needs along with creating barriers to their fulfillment.

The environmental problem descriptions below are presented in a social systems format influenced by Roland Warren's *The Community in America* (1963). Within the overarching system of the environment, Warren identified five subsystems which, when in existence in a community and operating effectively, create a climate of social well-being for members of the community. American society has not yet reached a level wherein its social institutions are capable of efficiently or effectively meeting the needs of its members. It is important, therefore, to identify the problems in those institutions and social systems, because they clearly impinge on the social functioning problems presented by social work clientele.

By clearly identifying a problem in the social system and environment, the social worker can make a considered decision about whether to intervene in the interpersonal problem, the environmental problem, or both. A social worker's client is likely to be experiencing some degree of difficulty in the social role and environmental areas; the clear delineation of each should facilitate the resolution or relief of the client's problems.

In the PIE system, six subsystems in the community have been selected in which environmental problem areas have been identified. Five of these have been drawn from Warren's conceptualization and the sixth (Affectional Support System) was added at the suggestion of social workers participating in the field testing of PIE. Those six subsystems are as follows:

1. *Economic/Basic Needs System:* The system of social institutions and social agencies that provides food, shelter, employment, funds, and transportation.

2. *Education and Training System:* The system of social institutions that transmits knowledge and skills, educates people about the values of the society, and serves in the development of skills that are needed to maintain the society.

3. *Judicial and Legal System:* The system of social institutions and social agencies that controls the social behavior of people.

4. *Health, Safety, and Social Services System:* The system of social institutions and social agencies that provides for health (including mental health), safety, and social services.

5. *Voluntary Association System:* The system of religious organizations and community social support groups that facilitates social and spiritual growth and development.

6. *Affectional Support System:* The system of friendships and acquaintances that constitutes a person's individual social support system.

In the adaptation of Warren's system to PIE, the following terms and codes were developed. In each of the six groupings a number of categories are listed; these identify the areas within the system whereby specific problems can be identified.

Environmental Systems	Codes
1. Economic/Basic Needs System	5000.XX
Food/Nutrition	5100.XX
Shelter	5200.XX
Employment	5300.XX
Economic Resources	5400.XX
Transportation	5500.XX
Discrimination in Economic/Basic Needs System	5600.XX
2. Education and Training System	6000.XX
Education and Training	6100.XX
Discrimination in Education/Training System	6200.XX
3. Judicial and Legal System	7000.XX
Justice and Legal	7100.XX
Discrimination in Judicial/Legal System	7200.XX
4. Health, Safety, and Social Services System	8000.XX
Health/Mental Health	8100.XX
Safety	8200.XX
Social Services	8300.XX
Discrimination in Health, Safety, and Social Services System	8400.XX
5. Voluntary Association System	9000.XX
Religion	9100.XX
Community Groups	9200.XX
Discrimination in Voluntary Association System	9300.XX

6. Affectional Support System	10000.XX
Affectional Support	10100.XX
Discrimination in Affectional Support System	10200.XX

Factor II: Problem Identification

As in Factor I, in Factor II each environmental problem or condition is identified with a brief written statement and a code number of four or five digits. Only the Severity and Duration Indexes are used on Factor II. The first digit (X ___ . ___), or pair of digits for the Affectional Support System (XX ___ . ___), indicates the general social system in which the problem occurs; and the third digit to the left of the decimal point (_ X ___ . ___) indicates the subcategory of the social system in which the problem occurs. The first and second digits to the left of the decimal point (___ XX. ___) indicate the specific problem within the subcategory. A problem with a lack of shelter available on a regular basis, for example, is an Economic/Basic Needs System Problem (5000.XX) which falls in the shelter subcategory (5200.XX). The specific code for this particular problem (lack of available shelter on a regular basis) is 5201.XX.

If the descriptions in a particular category do not represent the client situation, the social worker may choose the Other subcategory. The social worker should list the specific problem not covered by the other listings in the category.

The social worker should list only the Factor II problems that affect Factor I problems. There may be many other environmental problems known by the social worker, but only those relevant to a specific client are recorded. The notation of a problem in a category does not usually point to any maladaptive or socially unacceptable behavior on the part of the client; it most often points to a problem in that social system.

Definitions of System Problems

Economic/Basic Needs System: 5000.XX

The problems in the Economic/Basic Needs System category are those related to the production, distribution, and consumption functions of the society's economic system. Problems in this category consist of those related to meeting basic needs for food, shelter, and clothing as well as acquiring goods and services.

Food/Nutrition	**5100.XX**
Lack of food supply on a regular basis (for example, there is a drought)	5101.XX
Food supply inadequate for nutrition with potential threat to health (for example, there are no fresh vegetables or fruits)	5102.XX
Inadequate water supply, with threat to health (for example, only powdered infant formula is	5103.XX

available in a community with poor water system)

Other food/nutrition problem (specify) (for example, a food supply exists, but civil war prevents delivery) — 5104.XX

Shelter — **5200.XX**

Absence of shelter in a community on a regular basis (for example, there is no housing for poor people or those with low income) — 5201.XX

Inadequate or substandard housing in a community (for example, housing does not meet building and health codes) — 5202.XX

Other shelter problem (specify) (for example, shelter for homeless people is available only during the winter months) — 5203.XX

Employment — **5300.XX**

Unemployment due to lack of work in the community — 5301.XX

Underemployment (for example, only part-time or low-wage jobs exist in the community) — 5302.XX

Inappropriate employment (lack of socially and legally acceptable employment in the community, for example, dealing drugs is the only source of income available in the community) — 5303.XX

Other employment problem (specify) (for example, only dangerous employment in an unsafe chemical plant is available) — 5304.XX

Economic Resources — **5400.XX**

Insufficient economic resources in community to provide for client and dependents (for example, public assistance is inadequate to meet basic needs) — 5401.XX

Insufficient economic resources in community to provide for needed services beyond sustenance (for example, there is no public assistance for other necessary items, such as wheelchairs and child care) — 5402.XX

Regulatory barriers to economic resources (for example, the regulations for eligibility for general assistance are overly restrictive) — 5403.XX

Other economic resources problem (specify) (for example, public assistance checks are delayed or lost) — 5404.XX

Transportation — **5500.XX**

Lack of transportation to make client accessible to job, special services, or social services (for example, there is no public transportation system in the community) — 5501.XX

Other transportation problem (for example, the public transportation system does not run at night)	5502.XX
Discrimination	**5600.XX**
Age discrimination (for example, there is mandatory retirement at age 65)	5601.XX
Ethnicity, color, or language discrimination (for example, African Americans are not accepted for employment in a fire department)	5602.XX
Religious discrimination (for example, Orthodox Jews are required to work on Saturdays)	5603.XX
Sex discrimination (for example, men are promoted rather than qualified women)	5604.XX
Sexual orientation discrimination (for example, gay men and lesbians are denied entry into the military)	5605.XX
Lifestyle discrimination (for example, landlords will not rent to communes)	5606.XX
Noncitizen status discrimination (for example, landlords will not rent to undocumented workers)	5607.XX
Veteran status discrimination (for example, an employer is biased against Vietnam veterans)	5608.XX
Dependency status discrimination (for example, landlords will not rent to people on welfare)	5609.XX
Disability discrimination (for example, there are no wheelchair lifts on public buses)	5610.XX
Marital status discrimination (for example, married women are not given partnerships in law firms)	5611.XX
Other discrimination in Economic/Basic Needs System (specify) (for example, landlords will not rent to parents with young children)	5612.XX

Education and Training System Problems: 6000.XXX

The descriptions in the Education and Training System category are related to the goals of the educational system, which are to nurture intellectual development, cultivate work skills, and foster individual potential up to its optimal level. The barriers to reaching these goals are problems of access, discrimination, and cultural influence. Education is construed broadly, as either formal or informal and under either secular or religious auspices.

Education and Training	**6100.XX**
Lack of educational or training facilities (for example, there are no vocational training programs)	6101.XX
Lack of age-relevant, adequate, or appropriate educational or training facilities (for example,	6102.XX

there are no programs for adults who want to
earn high school diplomas)

Lack of culturally relevant educational or train-   6103.XX
ing opportunities (for example, there are no
vocational training programs for monolingual
Cantonese-speaking people)

Regulatory barriers to existing educational and   6104.XX
training services and programs (for example,
there are overly restrictive requirements to
qualify for vocational training programs)

Absence of support services needed to gain ac-   6105.XX
cess to educational/training opportunities (for
example, there is no child care at a vocational
college)

Other Education and Training System problem   6106.XX
(specify) (for example, a college library is not
open on the weekend)

Discrimination   **6200.XX**

Age discrimination (for example, people older   6201.XX
than 50 are not allowed to enter a training
program)

Ethnicity, color, or language discrimination (for   6202.XX
example, Asians are harassed at the police
academy)

Religious discrimination (for example, examina-   6203.XX
tions are scheduled on Jewish New Year)

Sex discrimination (for example, female students   6204.XX
have different dormitory curfew hours)

Sexual orientation discrimination (for example,   6205.XX
gay men and lesbians are not allowed to enter
the police academy)

Lifestyle discrimination (for example, children of   6206.XX
commune members are harassed at school)

Noncitizen status discrimination (for example, a   6207.XX
training program requires U.S. citizenship)

Veteran status discrimination (for example, mili-   6208.XX
tary training is not accepted as equivalent to
vocational training)

Dependency status discrimination (for example,   6209.XX
welfare clients are not accepted into a car re-
pair training course)

Disability discrimination (for example, a college   6210.XX
will not provide readers for blind students)

Marital status discrimination (for example, a hos-   6211.XX
pital will not accept married women for medi-
cal residencies)

Other Education and Training System discrimi-   6212.XX
nation (specify) (for example, social workers

are not accepted into a psychoanalytic training institute)

Judicial and Legal System Problems: 7000.XXX

The descriptions in the Judicial and Legal System category are derived from
the system's primary function of social control. Enforcement measures create closed environments, and ongoing compliance can generate special re-
stricted conditions.

Judicial and Legal	**7100.XX**
Lack of police services (for example, there is no police station in a small town)	7101.XX
Lack of relevant police services (for example, there is no sexual assault specialist)	7102.XX
Lack of confidence in police services (for example, police are thought to be slow to respond to emergency calls)	7103.XX
Lack of adequate prosecution or defense services (for example, there are not enough public defenders to handle the caseload)	7104.XX
Lack of adequate probation or parole services (for example, there is no work furlough program)	7105.XX
Other Judicial and Legal System problem (specify) (for example, judges are inadequately trained to handle child abuse cases)	7106.XX
Discrimination	**7200.XX**
Age discrimination (for example, there are no programs for older offenders)	7201.XX
Ethnicity, color, or language discrimination (for example, African Americans are harassed by the police)	7202.XX
Religious discrimination (for example, Sikhs are not allowed to become police officers)	7203.XX
Sex discrimination (for example, there are no halfway houses for female offenders)	7204.XX
Sexual orientation discrimination (for example, there are homophobic judges)	7205.XX
Lifestyle discrimination (for example, homeless people are harassed by police)	7206.XX
Noncitizen status discrimination (for example, public defenders will not defend noncitizens)	7207.XX
Veteran status discrimination (for example, Vietnam veterans are given more severe sentences by judges)	7208.XX
Dependency status discrimination (for example, welfare parents are more likely to have children taken away)	7209.XX

Disability discrimination (for example, deaf people cannot serve on juries)	7210.XX
Marital status discrimination (for example, only legally married prisoners may have conjugal visits)	7211.XX
Other Judicial and Legal System discrimination (for example, police will not arrest other police officers who commit crimes)	7212.XX

Health, Safety, and Social Services System Problems: 8000.XXX

The elements of the Health, Safety, and Social Services System are of the health, mental health, public safety, and social services delivery agencies and programs that provide service to those in need. The focus in this category is not on the health or other problems of the individual but on the existence and availability of services that sustain the health and welfare of the individual.

Health/Mental Health	**8100.XX**
Absence of adequate health services (for example, no AIDS testing is available)	8101.XX
Regulatory barriers to health services (for example, Medicare does not cover a needed health service)	8102.XX
Inaccessibility of health services (for example, dialysis is 100 miles away)	8103.XX
Absence of support services needed to use health services (for example, no child care is available during clinic hours)	8104.XX
Absence of adequate mental health services (for example, no day treatment is available)	8105.XX
Regulatory barriers to mental health services (for example, client does not meet residency criteria to receive outpatient services)	8106.XX
Inaccessibility of mental health services (for example, the community mental health clinic is 100 miles away)	8107.XX
Absence of support services needed to use mental health services (for example, no translator for case management services is available)	8101.XX
Other health/mental health services system problem (specify) (for example, a client's employer terminates health insurance because of excessive cost)	8109.XX
Safety	**8200.XX**
Violence or crime in neighborhood (for example, a client lives next to a crack house)	8201.XX
Unsafe working conditions (for example, a client works with toxic chemicals)	8202.XX

Unsafe conditions in home (for example, a house does not meet earthquake standards)	8203.XX
Absence of adequate safety services (for example, there is no fire department in a rural area)	8204.XX
Natural disaster of large proportions (for example, there is a major flood)	8205.XX
Human-created disaster (for example, a refinery explosion has occurred)	8206.XX
Other safety problem (specify) (for example, there are no stop signs at a busy intersection)	8207.XX
Social Services	**8300.XX**
Absence of adequate social services (for example, no homeless programs exist)	8301.XX
Regulatory barriers to social services (for example, a client cannot pass a means test)	8302.XX
Inaccessibility of social services (for example, a hot line for parents is not open on the weekend)	8303.XX
Absence of support services needed to use social services (for example, no case management is provided to a client in a parent education class)	8304.XX
Other social services problem (specify) (for example, a client cannot meet with a social worker because of the worker's huge caseload)	8305.XX
Discrimination	**8400.XX**
Age discrimination (for example, an adoption agency will not place children with older adults)	8401.XX
Ethnicity, color, or language discrimination (for example, no mental health services are available in Spanish)	8402.XX
Religious discrimination (for example, a hospital does not provide for Muslim patients)	8403.XX
Sex discrimination (for example, a residential treatment program excludes females)	8404.XX
Sexual orientation discrimination (for example, a hospital will not allow the partner of a gay man spousal visitation rights)	8405.XX
Lifestyle discrimination (for example, the welfare department harasses punk rockers)	8406.XX
Noncitizen status discrimination (for example, clients must prove citizenship to obtain social services)	8407.XX
Veteran status discrimination (for example, veterans are denied services because they are expected to obtain services through the Veterans Administration)	8408.XX

Dependency status (for example, physicians will not accept Medicaid)	8409.XX
Disability discrimination (for example, an agency does not have wheelchair ramps)	8410.XX
Marital status discrimination (for example, a religious social services agency will not provide services to divorced clients)	8411.XX
Other Health, Safety, and Social Services System discrimination (specify) (for example, a clinic will not serve people who have AIDS)	8412.XX

Voluntary Association System Problems: 9000.XXX

The Voluntary Association System encompasses the common ways that people satisfy needs for social participation outside of the family and the workplace—through voluntary association in organized or informal religious and community groups. Religious groups are defined as those formally organized around a belief system pertaining to an ultimate reality or deity and having a commitment to religious faith or observance. Community groups are composed of people with common interests or characteristics banded together for social exchange and support. Among these are social clubs and self-help organizations.

Religious Groups	**9100.XX**
Lack of religious group of choice (for example, there is no Catholic parish in a rural area)	9101.XX
Lack of community acceptance of religious values (for example, the community harasses Hare Krishnas)	9102.XX
Other religious group problem (specify) (for example, a religious group tries to recruit people who are not interested in being recruited)	9103.XX
Community Groups	**9200.XX**
Lack of community support group of choice (for example, there is no neighborhood watch group)	9201.XX
Lack of community acceptance of community group of choice (for example, Hell's Angels are refused service in a community)	9202.XX
Other community group problem (specify) (for example, community groups fight with one another)	9203.XX
Discrimination	**9300.XX**
Age discrimination (for example, a church does not have a group for seniors)	9301.XX
Ethnicity, color, or language discrimination (for example, the Roman Catholic church does not allow for a specialized Vietnamese church)	9302.XX
Religious discrimination (for example, nuns are not accepted as leaders of a community organization)	9303.XX

Sex discrimination (for example, women are not accepted as clergy)	9304.XX
Sexual orientation discrimination (for example, a religious denomination will not accept a gay or lesbian subgroup)	9305.XX
Lifestyle discrimination (for example, parents who live in a commune cannot join a parent cooperative)	9306.XX
Noncitizen status discrimination (for example, a community group requires citizenship status for membership)	9307.XX
Veteran status discrimination (for example, veterans are not accepted as members of an antiwar group)	9308.XX
Dependency status discrimination (for example, women on welfare are not accepted by a single-parent group)	9309.XX
Disability discrimination (for example, developmentally delayed people are not allowed into a church group)	9310.XX
Marital status discrimination (for example, single parents cannot join a parent cooperative)	9311.XX
Other Voluntary Association System discrimination (specify) (for example, police officers are not accepted into a peace group)	9312.XX

Affectional Support System Problems: 10000.XXX

The Affectional Support System is the network of social relationships in an individual's personal social support system. This system can consist of marital family, extended family, family of origin, friends, acquaintances, coworkers, paid or volunteer helpers, and service providers such as bartenders, beauticians, and police officers. The Affectional Support System includes everyone who has an affectional tie with the client. Problems in this system occur in the external system, not in the client's ability to access the system (which would be listed on Factor I instead).

Affectional Support	**10100.XX**
Absence of an affectional support system (for example, no friends, relatives, or acquaintances are available to a client)	10101.XX
Support system is inadequate to meet affectional needs of client (for example, friends, relatives, and acquaintances exist, but they are not able to provide emotional support to the client)	10102.XX
Excessively involved support system (for example, an overprotective family will not allow a disabled person to live independently)	10103.XX

Other Affectional Support System problem (specify) (for example, a client's Affectional Support System is mostly composed of alcoholics)	10104.XX
Discrimination	**10200.XX**
Age discrimination (for example, older members of the family are excluded from family events)	10201.XX
Ethnicity, color, or language discrimination (for example, a support system will not accept a client's spouse who is of a different race)	10202.XX
Religious discrimination (for example, the family rejects a client who married outside of the family's religion)	10203.XX
Sex discrimination (for example, a client's support system insists that a woman needs more support than a man because women are assumed to be weaker)	10204.XX
Sexual orientation discrimination (for example, a client's support system shuns a man who comes out as gay)	10205.XX
Lifestyle discrimination (for example, a client's support system shuns a woman who lives with an unmarried partner)	10206.XX
Noncitizen status discrimination (for example, coworkers reject a man when they find out he is not a citizen)	10207.XX
Veteran status discrimination (for example, a politically radical family refuses to provide housing for a son returning from fighting in an unpopular war)	10208.XX
Dependency status discrimination (for example, family members withdraw when a woman goes on welfare)	10209.XX
Disability discrimination (for example, a client's support system withdraws after he develops Parkinson's disease)	10210.XX
Marital status discrimination (for example, the support system rejects a recent widow)	10211.XX
Other Affectional Support System discrimination (specify) (for example, a woman is rejected by childless friends after she has a baby)	10212.XX

Reference

Warren, R. (1963). *The community in America.* Chicago: Rand McNally.

5.

Severity, Duration, and Coping Indexes

The practitioner should use the Severity, Coping, and Duration Indexes to amplify the assessment of the client's social functioning as recorded on Factors I and II. The Severity Index indicates the degree of change or transition experienced by the client. The Duration Index measures the recency and duration of the problem. The Coping Index gauges the internal resources available to the client for addressing the identified problems. The practitioner should use the three indexes to complete the description of the client's social functioning and environmental problems and to provide an indication of whether social work intervention is required.

Severity Index

The Severity Index is used on both Factors I and II. Change and transition are facts of everyday life, and thus changes in roles, relationships, and events characterize most cases that come to the attention of social workers. The practitioner should use the Severity Index to differentiate instances when change is extensive, rapid, and problem-producing from instances when change is less problematic for the client. The index has a six-point scale with 6 as the highest degree of severity and 1 as the lowest. When change is pervasive and highly disruptive, the need for social work intervention is probably high.

The severity indicator is coded to the right of the decimal point. Thus, if the problem on Factor I or II is rated as moderate in severity, it is noted as 3 in the first digit to the right of the decimal point (_____ .X __): for example, Factor I, 1110.3XX, Parent Role Problem, power type, moderate severity; or Factor II, 5101.3X, Economic/Basic Needs System Problem, lack of food supply on a regular basis, moderate severity.

The six levels of the Severity Index and their code numbers are

- *No problem* = 1
  The problem is perceived as nondisruptive by both the client and the practitioner. No intervention is needed.

- *Low severity* = 2
  The problem may include some change but is perceived as nondisruptive by the client, although disruption may be noted by the practitioner. Intervention may be desirable but not necessary. Examples include starting school, getting a traffic ticket, or having an argument with a neighbor.

- *Moderate severity* = 3
  The problem is disruptive to the client's functioning, but the distress is not judged as impairing general functioning. Intervention would be helpful. Examples include separating from a spouse, losing a job, or being a single parent.

- *High severity* = 4
  The problem involves fewer or less dramatic changes, but the client is in a clear state of distress. Early intervention is indicated. Examples include getting a divorce, major financial loss, or the death of a friend.

- *Very high severity* = 5
  The problem is characterized by changes in key or multiple areas of social role functioning or in the environment. Immediate intervention is probably necessary. Examples include the death of a spouse, serious illness, or rape.

- *Catastrophic* = 6
  The problem is characterized by sudden, negative changes out of the individual's control with devastating implications for adjustment. Immediate direct intervention is indicated. Problems of this severity are induced by events such as interment in a concentration camp, multiple family deaths, and loss of possessions in a natural disaster.

Duration Index

The Duration Index is used on Factors I and II. The Duration Index indicates the length or recency of the problem. Along with the Severity Index, it alerts the practitioner to the degree of urgency for intervention. Coupled with the Coping Index for Factor I problems, the Duration Index is a measure of the prognosis for problem resolution. For example, a client with good coping skills and a recently developed problem has a higher probability for problem resolution than a client with a chronic problem and poor coping skills.

The Duration Index rating can range from two weeks or less, rated as 6, to more than five years, rated as 1. It is recorded on the second digit to the right of the decimal point (_____ . _ X_) on both Factor I and II. Thus, if the problem on Factor I or II is rated as having a duration of three months, it is noted as 4 in the second digit to the right of the decimal point. For example, Factor I, 1110.34X, Parent Role Problem, power type, moderate severity, one to six months duration; or Factor II, 5101.45 Economic/Basic Needs System Problem, lack of food supply on a regular basis, high severity, two weeks' to one month's duration.

The six levels of the Duration Index and their code numbers are

- more than five years = 1
- one to five years = 2
- six months to one year = 3
- one to six months = 4
- two to four weeks = 5
- two weeks or less = 6.

Coping Index

The Coping Index is used only on Factor I. This indicator is a measure of
the client's ability to manage a problem with his or her own internal resources. The Coping Index consists of the social worker's rating of the client's ability to solve problems, capacity to act independently, and his or her
ego strength, insight, and intellectual capacity. In doing so the practitioner
is assessing the client's positive social role functioning. Social work intervention is most needed when the client lacks adequate coping skills.

The Coping Index ratings range from no coping skills, coded as 6, to outstanding coping skills, coded as 1. The rating is noted on the third digit to
the right of the decimal point (_____.___ X). Thus, if a client's coping skills
are rated as inadequate, it is coded as 5 in the third place to the right of the
decimal point. For example, Factor I, 1110.345, Parent Role Problem, power
type, moderate severity, one to six months duration, inadequate coping
skills. The six levels of the Coping Index and their code numbers are

- *Outstanding coping skills* = 1
  The client's ability to solve problems, act independently, and to use ego
  strength, insight, and intellectual ability to cope with difficult situations is
  exceptional.

- *Above-average coping skills* = 2
  The client's ability to solve problems, act independently, and to use ego
  strength, insight, and intellectual ability to cope with difficult situations is
  more than would be expected in the average person.

- *Adequate coping skills* = 3
  The client is able to solve problems, act independently, and has adequate
  ego strength, insight, and intellectual ability.

- *Somewhat inadequate coping skills* = 4
  The client has fair problem-solving ability but has major difficulties solving the presenting problems, acting independently, and using ego
  strength, insight, or intellectual ability.

- *Inadequate coping skills* = 5
  The client has some ability to solve problems but it is insufficient to solve
  the presenting problems; the client shows poor ability to act independently; and the client has minimal ego strength, insight, and intellectual
  ability.

- *No coping skills* = 6
  The client shows little or no ability to solve problems, lacks the capacity to
  act independently, and has insufficient ego strength, insight, and intellectual ability.

6.

Case Examples Using PIE in Various Agency Settings

The following case vignettes are intended to illustrate the PIE assessment process and the coding system as applied in the following settings.

Family Services Agency

A 23-year-old single mother comes into the family services agency where you work. Using your routine method of assessment, you determine that her primary problem is the difficulty she is having in dealing with the responsibilities of being a parent (Parent Role Problem, responsibility type, 1130.XXX), and that a secondary problem is her ambivalent relationship with her boyfriend (Lover Role Problem, ambivalence type, 2120.XXX). For her Parent Role Problem, you determine that the disruption it causes is moderate (3), the duration is one to five years (2), and her coping capacity is somewhat inadequate (4), because she has made no headway in resolving this problem. For her Lover Role problem, you determine that the disruption it causes is low (2), the duration rating is one to six months (4) because the problem has been going on for three months, and her coping capacity is judged by you as somewhat inadequate (4). Thus, this client's Factor I statement would appear as follows:

Factor I 130.324 Parent Role Problem, responsibility type, moderate severity, one-to-five years' duration, somewhat inadequate coping capacity (primary problem)

2120.244 Lover Role Problem, ambivalence type, low severity, one- to six-months' duration, somewhat inadequate coping capacity

You determine that the client's difficulties are compounded because there is no work available and she is not eligible for public assistance. You identify this as an Economic/Basic Needs System Problem, lack of economic resources to provide for herself and her dependents (5401.XX). You judge this as causing a high degree of disruption (4). You determine that the community's economic problems have been going on for three weeks, because a major industry closed and the government is in a financial crisis. The duration rating is 5. Thus, this client's Factor II statement would appear as follows:

Factor II 5401.45 Economic/Basic Needs System Problem, insufficient economic resources in the community to provide for client and dependents, high severity, two- to four-weeks' duration

You determine that this client is depressed and meets the criteria for a single episode of Major Depression as described in the *Diagnostic and Statistical Manual of Mental Disorders, Fourth Edition* (DSM-IV) (American Psychiatric Association, 1994). You determine that she does not have a personality disorder or developmental problem. Therefore, this client's Factor III statement would appear as follows:

Factor III
    Axis I   296.22   Major Depression, single episode, moderate
    Axis II   V71.09   No diagnosis on Axis II

Finally, the client reports no physical conditions or disorders affecting her Factor I and II problems. Therefore, Factor IV would be recorded as follows:

Factor IV   0000.00   No problem (by client report)

The complete multifactorial description of this client on PIE follows:

Factor I	1130.324	Parent Role Problem, responsibility type, moderate severity, one to five years' duration, somewhat inadequate coping capacity (primary problem)
	2120.244	Lover Role Problem, ambivalence type, low severity, one to six months' duration, somewhat inadequate coping capacity
Factor II	5401.45	Economic/Basic Needs System Problem, insufficient economic resources in the community to provide for self and dependents, high severity, two to four weeks' duration

Factor III
    Axis I   296.22   Major Depression, single episode, moderate
    Axis II   V71.09   No diagnosis on Axis II

Factor IV   0000.00   No problem (by client report)

Criminal Justice

A 45-year-old ex-offender on parole is referred to the community agency where you work. After serving five years in prison he is dealing with the change he is experiencing from that of prisoner to parolee (4450.XXX). You observe that this status change or loss is causing a high degree of anxiety in the client (4). You learn that he was released from prison three days before, so the duration rating is 2 weeks or less (6), and from what you know of his history you judge his coping skills to be adequate (3). This client's Factor I statement would be written as follows:

Factor I	4450.463	Probationer/Parolee Role Problem, loss type, high severity, less than two weeks' duration, adequate coping skills

Although the community has many problems related to the economic system, such as inadequate food supplies, housing, and transportation, you conclude that the main economic system problem is the discrimination against parolees in obtaining adequate employment (5612.XX). This problem is of high severity in this community (4) and has been going on for many years (1). Thus, this client's Factor II statement would read as follows:

Factor II   5612.41   Economic/Basic Needs System Problem, discrimination, other discrimination (parole status), high severity, more than five years' duration

You determine that this client does not suffer from a mental, personality, or developmental disorder. Thus, his Factor III statement would appear as follows:

Factor III
   Axis I   V71.09   No diagnosis on Axis I
   Axis II   V71.09   No diagnosis on Axis II

Finally, the client's medical record reports that he has severe asthma, which worsens when he is under stress. Thus, his Factor IV statement would be the following:

Factor IV   Severe asthma (by Dr. X)

A complete multifactorial description of this client would be written as follows:

Factor I   4450.463   Probationer/Parolee Role Problem, loss type, high severity, less than two weeks' duration, adequate coping skills

Factor II   5612.41   Economic/Basic Needs System Problem, discrimination, other discrimination (parole status), high severity, more than five years' duration

Factor III
   Axis I   V71.09   No diagnosis on Axis I
   Axis II   V71.09   No diagnosis on Axis II

Factor IV   Severe asthma (by Dr. X)

Medical Social Work

A 25-year-old gay man has been admitted with a diagnosis of AIDS to the hospital where you work. Because of his illness, he has lost his job (3150.XXX) and has also been forced to reveal his homosexuality to his parents, which has resulted in his being unsure whether they accept him as their son (1320.XXX). You judge that this situation is causing a very high degree of disruption in his life (5) for both his paid Worker Role–Paid Economy and Child Role Problems. The loss of his job and the disclosure to his parents occurred within the past three weeks, so the duration rating is 5. You determine that his coping skills for both his Worker Role and Child

Role Problems are adequate, so his coping rating is 3 for each. This client's Factor I statement would be written as follows:

| Factor I | 3150.553 | Worker Role–Paid Economy Problem, loss type, very high severity, two to four weeks' duration, adequate coping skills (primary problem) |
| | 1320.553 | Child Role Problem, ambivalence type, very high severity, two to four weeks' duration, adequate coping skills |

Because of his illness no employment is available to him nor is he eligible for health insurance; the client no longer is able to support himself or his medical care, and there are no programs in the community to provide either financial aid or health care (5401.XX). This problem is causing a very high degree of anxiety (5), and the duration rating is again two to four weeks (5). Therefore, this client's Factor II statement would be written as follows:

| Factor II | 5401.55 | Economic/Basic Needs System Problem, insufficient community resources to provide for client, very high severity, two to four weeks' duration |

This client is severely depressed because of his life situation. He does not have a personality or developmental disorder. Therefore, his Factor III statement would be written as follows:

Factor III		
Axis I	296.23	Major Depression, single episode, severe
Axis II	V71.09	No diagnosis on Axis II

This man's Factor IV listing would be

| Factor IV | | AIDS (by Dr. Y) |

A complete multifactorial PIE report on this client would appear as follows:

Factor I	3150.553	Worker Role–Paid Economy Problem, loss type, very high severity, two to four weeks' duration, adequate coping skills (primary problem)
	1320.553	Child Role Problem, ambivalence type, very high severity, two to four weeks' duration, adequate coping skills
Factor II	5401.55	Economic/Basic Needs System Problem, insufficient community resources to provide for client, very high severity, two to four weeks' duration
Factor III		
Axis I	296.23	Major Depression, single episode, severe
Axis II	V71.09	No diagnosis on Axis II
Factor IV		AIDS (by Dr. Y)

Psychiatric Inpatient

In the psychiatric inpatient unit where you are employed, you are assigned to work with a 57-year-old woman who has been in and out of the mental health system many times in the past 40 years. She refers to the hospital as her home and has never been able to survive outside of an institutional setting for very long. But, because of the commitment laws and the cutbacks in state services, it has not been possible to keep her in the hospital for an extended stay. She constantly engages in behavior, most recently wandering in and out of traffic, that causes her to be rehospitalized. Because of the risk that she might be injured or killed, you determine that this woman's Inpatient/Client Role Problem (4240.XX) is of very high severity (5), the problem has been going on for 40 years, so the duration is more than five years (1), and you determine that she has no coping skills (6). This client's Factor I statement would be written as follows:

Factor I   4240.516   Inpatient/Client Role Problem, dependency type, very high severity, more than five years' duration, no coping skills

You determine that this client's problem is affected by lack of adequate mental health services available in her community outside of an institutional setting (8105.XX) and that the laws make it difficult to protect her (8102.XX). You determine that these Health, Safety, and Social Services System Problems are both of high severity (4) and have been going on for many years, so the duration is more than five years (1). Therefore, her Factor II statement would appear as follows:

Factor II   8105.41   Health, Safety, and Social Services System Problem, absence of adequate mental health services, high severity, more than five years' duration

8102.41   Health, Safety, and Social Services System Problem, regulatory barriers, high severity, more than five years' duration

As the result of a mental status examination, you determine that this client is suffering from chronic paranoid schizophrenia. She does not have a personality or developmental disorder. Therefore, her Factor III statement would be written as follows:

Factor III
  Axis I   295.32   Schizophrenia, paranoid type, chronic
  Axis II   V71.09   No diagnosis on Axis II

A physical examination reveals that this client has scabies and diabetes. Therefore, this client's Factor IV statement would appear as follows:

Factor IV   Diabetes (by Dr. Z)
             Scabies (by Dr. Z)

A complete multifactorial report on this client would appear as follows:

Factor I	4240.416	Inpatient/Client Role Problem, dependency type, very high severity, more than five years' duration, no coping skills
Factor II	8105.41	Health, Safety, and Social Services System Problem, absence of adequate mental health services, high severity, more than five years' duration
	8102.41	Health, Safety, and Social Services System Problem, regulatory barriers, high severity, more than five years' duration

Factor III
| Axis I | 295.32 | Schizophrenia, paranoid type, chronic |
| Axis II | V71.09 | No diagnosis on Axis II |

| Factor IV | | Diabetes (by Dr. Z) |
| | | Scabies (by Dr. Z) |

Public Assistance

An 18-year-old pregnant single mother of two comes to the welfare department where you are employed to apply for public assistance. She presents her main problem as being overwhelmed with the responsibility of caring for her two children. You assess this client's Parent Role Problem (1130.XXX) as causing her a moderate degree of anxiety (3); that the problem has been going on for two years, so the duration is one to five years (2); and that her coping skills are somewhat inadequate (4). Therefore, this client's Factor I statement would appear as follows:

| Factor I | 1130.324 | Parent Role Problem, responsibility type, moderate severity, one to five years' duration, somewhat inadequate coping skills |

Because this client must care for her young children and did not finish high school, she is unable to support herself and her children and she is therefore applying for public assistance, which provides less money than she needs to live on (5401.XX). Again, you determine that her environmental problem is causing a moderate degree of disruption (3) and that its duration is one to five years (2). Therefore, this client's Factor II statement would appear as follows:

| Factor II | 5401.32 | Economic/Basic Needs System Problem, insufficient economic resources to provide for client and dependents, moderate severity, one to five years' duration |

You determine that your client does not suffer from a mental, personality, or developmental disorder, so her Factor III statement would appear as follows:

Factor III
| Axis I | V71.09 | No diagnosis on Axis I |

Axis II   V71.09   No diagnosis on Axis II

Your client reports no physical conditions that affect her Factor I and II conditions. Therefore, her Factor IV statement would be written as follows:

Factor IV   No problem (by client report)

A complete multifactorial PIE report for his client would be presented as follows:

Factor I   1130.324   Parent Role Problem, responsibility type, moderate severity, one to five years' duration, somewhat inadequate coping skills

Factor II   5401.32   Economic/Basic Needs System Problem, insufficient economic resources to provide for client and dependents, moderate severity, one to five years' duration

Factor III
  Axis I   V71.09   No diagnosis on Axis I
  Axis II   V71.09   No diagnosis on Axis II

Factor IV   No problem (by client report)

Rehabilitation

You work in a rehabilitation facility for adults who have suffered spinal cord injury. You have been working with a 37-year-old man who was in a recent car accident and is now paraplegic. Although your client seems to be progressing well in the program, his wife presents to you her many concerns about her marriage in relation to her husband's disability. After you interview her, you determine that she has a Spouse Role Problem, as she defines her concern that her husband will no longer be the same man and she will lose the relationship she had with him (1250.XXX). You determine that this problem is causing a moderate disruption to the wife (3); that this problem has been going on for three months, so the duration rating would be one to six months (4); and that she has above average coping skills (2). This woman's Factor I statement would then appear as follows:

Factor I   1250.342   Spouse Role Problem, loss type, moderate severity, one to six months' duration, above-average coping skills

You determine that there are no environmental conditions that affect this woman's Spouse Role Problem, so her Factor II statement would be noted as follows:

Factor II   0000.00   No problem

You determine that this client is suffering from a Dependent Personality Disorder but no other mental or developmental disorder, so her Factor III statement would be described as follows:

Factor III
    Axis I   V71.09   No diagnosis on Axis I
    Axis II   301.60   Dependent Personality Disorder

She reports no physical conditions that affect her Factor I problem, so her Factor IV statement would be written as follows:

Factor IV   0000.00   No problem (by client report)

A complete multifactorial PIE report on this client would then be written as follows:

Factor I   1250.342   Spouse Role Problem, loss type, moderate severity, one to six months' duration, above-average coping skills

Factor II   0000.00   No problem

Factor III
    Axis I   V71.09   No diagnosis on Axis I
    Axis II   301.60   Dependent Personality Disorder

Factor IV   0000.00   No problem (by client report)

Outpatient Psychiatric Clinic

A 29-year-old man requests treatment at the outpatient psychiatric clinic where you work. He has been unemployed for four years, with no job prospects in sight (3150.XXX). His unemployment is causing a high disruption in his life (4). He has been unemployed for four years, so his duration is one to five years (2). You determine that his coping skills are inadequate (5). This man's Factor I statement would appear as follows:

Factor I   3150.425   Worker Role–Paid Economy Problem, loss type, high severity, one to five years' duration, inadequate coping skills

This man's unemployment benefits ran out years ago; and he has been surviving on public assistance, but unfortunately, the job picture in his community is dismal (5301.XX). Again, this situation is causing a high degree of disruption (4), and the duration is one to five years (2). This man's Factor II statement would be described as follows:

Factor II   5301.42   Economic/Basic Needs System Problem, unemployment, high severity, one to five years' duration

Your client is severely depressed and reveals to you that he is contemplating suicide. In addition, he has been drinking three bottles of cheap wine every day for the past several years. He does not meet the criteria for a personality or developmental disorder. His Factor III statement would be written as follows:

Factor III
   Axis I   296.23   Major Depression, single episode, severe (principal diagnosis)
               303.90   Alcohol Dependence
   Axis II   V71.09   No diagnosis on Axis II

The results of his physical examination reveal that your client has cirrhosis of the liver. His Factor IV would be described as follows:

Factor IV   Cirrhosis of the liver (by Dr. Z)

This client's complete PIE description would appear as follows:

Factor I   3150.425   Worker Role–Paid Economy Problem, loss type, high severity, one to five years' duration, inadequate coping skills

Factor II   5301.42   Economic/Basic Needs System Problem, unemployment, high severity, one to five years' duration

Factor III
   Axis I   296.23   Major Depression, single episode, severe (principal diagnosis)
               303.90   Alcohol Dependence
   Axis II   V71.09   No diagnosis on Axis II

Factor IV   Cirrhosis of the liver (by Dr. Z)

Private Practice

A middle-aged married couple, both attorneys, are referred to you by their physician for help with marital problems. Their presenting problem is that their marriage has "gone dead." They are no longer able to communicate and are having sexual problems. This Spouse Role Problem (1230.XXX) is causing a moderate disruption (3) to each member of this couple. Their problem has been going on for nine months, so its duration is six months to one year (3). You determine that each member of the couple has above-average coping skills (2). The Factor I description for each member of this couple would appear as follows:

Factor I   1230.332   Spouse Role Problem, responsibility type, moderate severity, six months' to one year's duration, above-average coping skills

You determine that there are no environmental factors affecting their Spouse Role Problem, so each spouse's Factor II statement would appear as follows:

Factor II   0000.00   No problem

Neither has a mental disorder, but the husband has a Narcissistic Personality Disorder. The husband's Factor III statement would be described as follows:

Factor III
    Axis I   V71.09   No diagnosis on Axis I
    Axis II   301.81   Narcissistic Personality Disorder

The wife's Factor III statement would be described as follows:

Factor III
    Axis I   V71.09   No diagnosis on Axis I
    Axis II   V71.09   No diagnosis on Axis II

They report no physical conditions that affect their Spouse Role Problem, so each spouse's Factor IV statement would be written as follows:

Factor IV   No problem (by client report)

A complete multifactorial PIE report on the husband would appear as follows:

Factor I   1230.332   Spouse Role Problem, responsibility type, moderate severity, six months' to one year's duration, above-average coping skills

Factor II   0000.00   No problem

Factor III
    Axis I   V71.09   No diagnosis on Axis I
    Axis II   301.81   Narcissistic Personality Disorder

Factor IV   No problem (by client report)

A complete multifactorial PIE report on the wife would appear as follows:

Factor I   1230.332   Spouse Role Problem, responsibility type, moderate severity, six months' to one year's duration, above-average coping skills

Factor II   0000.00   No problem

Factor III
    Axis I   V71.09   No diagnosis on Axis I
    Axis II   V71.09   No diagnosis on Axis II

Factor IV   No problem (by client report)

Developmental Disabilities

You work in a regional center for developmentally delayed individuals. A long-term client of the center, a 45-year-old woman with autism, has lived with her widowed mother all her life, but one week ago her mother died. You determine that the loss of the client's mother is causing a Child Role Problem, loss type (1350.XXX). This problem is of high severity (4), the duration is two weeks or less (6), and your client has inadequate coping skills (5). This client's Factor I statement would appear as follows:

Factor I 1350.465 Child Role Problem, loss type, high severity, two weeks' or less duration, inadequate coping skills

No one else in your client's family can take her in, and there is no opening in the one group home in your community. You rated this client's Health, Safety, and Social Services System Problem (8301.XX) as high (4), and you determine that there has always been a severe lack of group homes available for developmentally delayed individuals in your community, so the duration is more than five years (1). This woman's Factor II statement would appear as follows:

Factor II 8301.41 Health, Safety, and Social Services System Problem, absence of adequate social services, high severity, more than five years' duration

Your client does not have a mental or personality disorder, but she does have the developmental disorder of autism so her Factor III would appear as follows:

Factor III
  Axis I   V71.09   No diagnosis
  Axis II 290.00   Autistic Disorder

Your client has no physical disorder that is affecting her current situation, so her Factor IV statement would appear as follows:

Factor IV   None reported by family members

A complete multifactorial PIE report on this client would appear as follows:

Factor I 1350.465 Child Role Problem, loss type, high severity, two weeks' or less duration, inadequate coping skills

Factor II 8301.41 Health, Safety, and Social Services System Problem, absence of adequate social services, high severity, more than five years' duration

Factor III
  Axis I   V71.09   No diagnosis
  Axis II 299.00   Autistic Disorder

Factor IV   None reported by family members

Reference

American Psychiatric Association. (1994). *Diagnostic and statistical manual of mental disorders* (4th ed.). Washington, DC: American Psychiatric Press.

7.

The Mini-PIE

For the experienced user, the Mini-PIE is a concise, easy way to record the results of a PIE assessment. We are very grateful for the help of Cheryl Cohen of the New York State Psychiatric Institute and Cathy Beckwith, an MSW student at the University of Utah, for working on earlier versions of the Mini-PIE. We are especially grateful to Elizabeth Irvin of the Commonwealth of Massachusetts Department of Mental Health for her extensive work on this final version.

After the Assessment: Writing Up the Client's Problems Using the Mini-PIE

Factor I

1. Identify all the social relationships with which the client is currently having difficulty (for example, with spouse—Spousal Role Problem; with employer—Occupational Role Problem). If there is more than one problem relationship, identify them as primary, secondary, and so forth.

2. For each social relationship problem, identify the primary type (for example, person loses spouse by death or divorce—Spousal Role Problem, loss type). If you have difficulty choosing between two, list both, underlining the one that is most likely primary. If you identify three or more problems, use the mixed category.

3. For each problem, identify its severity as perceived by you on a scale from 2 = low to 6 = catastrophic. A 1 indicates no problem perceived by you or the client.

4. For each problem, identify the length of time since onset on a scale from 1 = five years or more to 6 = most recent (to match Severity Index).

5. For each problem, identify your estimate of the client's ability to cope with it on a scale from 1 = the client would most likely deal with the problem with little or no help to 6 = the client has no ability to deal with the problem without help.

Factor II

1. Identify the problems outside the individual—in the social institutions, in the community, and in the social networks in the client's environment—that are considered by the soical worker as related to or affecting social relationships.

2. Identify the social system in which the problem exists (for example, the client has no place to live—Economic/Basic Needs System Problem; the client has no close friends—Affectional Support System Problem).

3. Identify the type of social system problem (for example, the client has no place to live because there is no suitable housing available—Economic/Basic Needs System Problem, absence of shelter in a community; the client has no friends—Affectional Support System Problem, absence of an affectional support system).

4. Identify the severity of the problem on a scale from 1 = lowest to 6 = highest.

5. Identify the length of time the problem is thought to have existed on a scale from 1 = five years or longer to 6 = two weeks or less.

Factor III
1. List the DSM Axis I diagnosis.
2. List the DSM Axis II diagnosis.

Factor IV
1. List the medical diagnosis along with the source of diagnosis.

1–4. FACTOR I:
PROBLEMS IN SOCIAL FUNCTIONING

Client Name: _____

Interview Date: ____ / ____ / ____

Evaluator: _____

1.	FAMILIAL ROLES	Code	Type	Severity	Duration	Coping	Recommended Intervention
☐	Parent	11					
☐	Spouse	12					
☐	Child	13					
☐	Sibling	14					
☐	Other Family Member	15					
☐	Significant Other	16					

2.	OTHER INTERPERSONAL ROLES	Code	Type	Severity	Duration	Coping	Recommended Intervention
☐	Lover	21					
☐	Friend	22					
☐	Neighbor	23					
☐	Member	24					
☐	Other (specify):	25					

3.	OCCUPATIONAL ROLES	Code	Type	Severity	Duration	Coping	Recommended Intervention
☐	Worker–Paid Economy	31					
☐	Worker–Home	32					
☐	Worker–Volunteer	33					
☐	Student	34					
☐	Other (specify):	35					

4.	SPECIAL LIFE SITUATION ROLES	Code	Type	Severity	Duration	Coping	Recommended Intervention
☐	Consumer	41					
☐	Inpatient/Client	42					
☐	Outpatient/Client	43					
☐	Probationer/Parolee	44					
☐	Prisoner	45					
☐	Immigrant–Legal	46					
☐	Immigrant–Undocumented	47					
☐	Immigrant–Refugee	48					
☐	Other (specify):	49					

☐	NO SOCIAL INTERACTION PROBLEMS	0000					

TYPE OF SOCIAL INTERACTION PROBLEM
10 Power
20 Ambivalence
30 Responsibility
40 Dependency
50 Loss
60 Isolation
70 Victimization
80 Mixed
90 Other (specify) _____

SEVERITY INDEX
1 No Problem   4 High
2 Low   5 Very high
3 Moderate   6 Catastrophic

DURATION INDEX
1 More than five years
2 One to five years
3 Six months to one year
4 One to six months
5 Two weeks to one month
6 Less than two weeks

COPING INDEX
1 Outstanding
2 Above average
3 Adequate
4 Somewhat inadequate
5 Inadequate
6 No coping skills

© 1994, NASW Press, Washington, DC

5. FACTOR II: PROBLEMS IN THE ENVIRONMENT

ECONOMIC/BASIC NEEDS SYSTEM PROBLEMS

FOOD/NUTRITION	Code	Severity	Duration	Recommended Intervention
☐ Lack of regular food supply	5101			
☐ Nutritionally inadequate food supply	5102			
☐ Documented malnutrition	5103			
☐ Other (specify):	5104			

SHELTER	Code	Severity	Duration	Recommended Intervention
☐ Absence of shelter	5201			
☐ Substandard or inadequate shelter	5202			
☐ Other (specify):	5203			

EMPLOYMENT	Code	Severity	Duration	Recommended Intervention
☐ Unemployment Employment not available in community	5301			
☐ Underemployment Adequate employment not available in community	5302			
☐ Inappropriate employment Lack of socially/legally acceptable employment in community	5303			
☐ Other (specify):	5304			

ECONOMIC RESOURCES	Code	Severity	Duration	Recommended Intervention
☐ Insufficient community resources for basic sustenance (self/dependent)	5401			
☐ Insufficient resources in community to provide for needed services beyond sustenance	5402			
☐ Regulatory barriers to economic resources	5403			
☐ Other (specify):	5404			

TRANSPORTATION	Code	Severity	Duration	Recommended Intervention
☐ No personal/public transportation to job/needed services	5501			
☐ Other (specify):	5502			

DISCRIMINATION	Code	Severity	Duration	Recommended Intervention
☐ If applicable, select discrimination type from list below. Write code in box to right.	56_ _			

NO PROBLEMS IN ECONOMIC/ BASIC NEEDS SYSTEM	0000			
☐				

DISCRIMINATION CODES

01 Age	07 Noncitizen
02 Ethnicity, color, or language	08 Veteran status
	09 Dependency status
03 Religion	10 Disability status
04 Sex	11 Marital status
05 Sexual orientation	12 Other (please specify):
06 Lifestyle	_____

SEVERITY INDEX

1 No problem
2 Low
3 Moderate
4 High
5 Very high
6 Catastrophic

DURATION INDEX

1 More than five years
2 One to five years
3 Six months to one year
4 One to six months
5 Two weeks to one month
6 Less than two weeks

6. EDUCATION AND TRAINING SYSTEM

	EDUCATION AND TRAINING	Code	Severity	Duration	Recommended Intervention
☐	Lack of educational/training facilities	6101			
☐	Lack of age-relevant, adequate, or appropriate educational/training facilities	6102			
☐	Lack of culturally relevant educational/training opportunities	6103			
☐	Regulatory barriers to existing educational/training services and programs	6104			
☐	Absence of support services needed to access educational/training opportunities	6105			
☐	Other (specify):	6106			

	DISCRIMINATION	Code	Severity	Duration	Recommended Intervention
☐	If applicable, select discrimination type from list below. Write code in box to right.	62_ _			

		Code			
☐	**NO PROBLEMS IN EDUCATION/ TRAINING SYSTEM**	**0000**			

7. JUDICIAL AND LEGAL SYSTEM

	JUSTICE AND LEGAL SYSTEM	Code	Severity	Duration	Recommended Intervention
☐	Lack of police services	7101			
☐	Lack of relevant police services	7102			
☐	Lack of confidence in police services	7103			
☐	Lack of adequate prosecution/defense services	7104			
☐	Lack of adequate probation/parole services	7105			
☐	Other (specify):	7106			

	DISCRIMINATION	Code	Severity	Duration	Recommended Intervention
☐	If applicable, select discrimination type from list below. Write code in box to right.	72_ _			

		Code			
☐	**NO PROBLEMS IN JUDICIAL/LEGAL SYSTEM**	**0000**			

DISCRIMINATION CODES
01 Age
02 Ethnicity, color, or language
03 Religion
04 Sex
05 Sexual orientation
06 Lifestyle
07 Noncitizen
08 Veteran status
09 Dependency status
10 Disability status
11 Marital status
12 Other (please specify):
_____

SEVERITY INDEX
1 No problem
2 Low
3 Moderate
4 High
5 Very high
6 Catastrophic

DURATION INDEX
1 More than five years
2 One to five years
3 Six months to one year
4 One to six months
5 Two weeks to one month
6 Less than two weeks

8. HEALTH, SAFETY, AND SOCIAL SERVICES SYSTEM

HEALTH / MENTAL HEALTH		Code	Severity	Duration	Recommended Intervention
☐	Absence of adequate health services	8101			
☐	Regulatory barriers to health services	8102			
☐	Inaccessibility of health services	8103			
☐	Absence of support services needed to use health services (child care, translator)	8104			
☐	Absence of adequate mental health services	8105			
☐	Regulatory barriers to mental health services	8106			
☐	Inaccessibility of mental health services	8107			
☐	Absence of support services needed to use mental health services	8108			
☐	Other (specify):	8109			

SAFETY		Code	Severity	Duration	Recommended Intervention
☐	Violence or crime in neighborhood	8201			
☐	Unsafe working conditions	8202			
☐	Unsafe conditions in home	8203			
☐	Absence of adequate safety services	8204			
☐	Natural disaster	8205			
☐	Human-created disaster	8206			
☐	Other (specify):	8207			

SOCIAL SERVICES		Code	Severity	Duration	Recommended Intervention
☐	Absence of adequate social services	8301			
☐	Regulatory barriers to social services	8302			
☐	Inaccessibility of social services	8303			
☐	Absence of support services needed to use social services (child care, transport)	8304			
☐	Other (specify):	8305			

DISCRIMINATION		Code	Severity	Duration	Recommended Intervention
☐	If applicable, select discrimination type from list below. Write code in box to right.	84_ _			

| ☐ | NO PROBLEMS IN HEALTH, SAFETY, AND SOCIAL SERVICES SYSTEM | 0000 | | | |

DISCRIMINATION CODES

01 Age	07 Noncitizen
02 Ethnicity, color, or language	08 Veteran status
	09 Dependency status
03 Religion	10 Disability status
04 Sex	11 Marital status
05 Sexual orientation	12 Other (please specify):
06 Lifestyle	_____

SEVERITY INDEX

1 No problem
2 Low
3 Moderate
4 High
5 Very high
6 Catastrophic

DURATION INDEX

1 More than five years
2 One to five years
3 Six months to one year
4 One to six months
5 Two weeks to one month
6 Less than two weeks

9. VOLUNTARY ASSOCIATION SYSTEM

	RELIGIOUS GROUPS	Code	Severity	Duration	Recommended Intervention
❐	Lack of religious group of choice	9101			
❐	Lack of community acceptance of religious values	9102			
❐	Other (specify):	9103			

	COMMUNITY GROUPS	Code	Severity	Duration	Recommended Intervention
❐	Lack of community support group of choice	9201			
❐	Lack of community acceptance of community group of choice	9202			
❐	Other (specify):	9203			

	DISCRIMINATION IN VOLUNTARY ASSOCIATION SYSTEM	Code	Severity	Duration	Recommended Intervention
❐	If applicable, select discrimination type from list below. Write code in box to right.	93_ _			

❐	**NO PROBLEM IN VOLUNTARY ASSOCIATION SYSTEM**	0000	

10. AFFECTIONAL SUPPORT SYSTEM

	AFFECTIONAL SUPPORT	Code	Severity	Duration	Recommended Intervention
❐	Absence of affectional support system	10101			
❐	Support system inadequate to meet affectional needs	10102			
❐	Excessively involved support system	10103			
❐	Other (specify):	10104			

	DISCRIMINATION IN AFFECTIONAL SUPPORT SYSTEM	Code	Severity	Duration	Recommended Intervention
❐	If applicable, select discrimination type from list below. Write code in box to right.	102_ _			

❐	**NO PROBLEMS IN AFFECTIONAL SUPPORT SYSTEM**	0000	

DISCRIMINATION CODES

01 Age	07 Noncitizen
02 Ethnicity, color, or language	08 Veteran status
	09 Dependency status
03 Religion	10 Disability status
04 Sex	11 Marital status
05 Sexual orientation	12 Other (please specify):
06 Lifestyle	_____

SEVERITY INDEX

1 No problem
2 Low
3 Moderate
4 High
5 Very high
6 Catastrophic

DURATION INDEX

1 More than five years
2 One to five years
3 Six months to one year
4 One to six months
5 Two weeks to one month
6 Less than two weeks

Factor I and Factor II Worksheet

Case: _____   Evaluator: _____

Date: _____

Factor I   Social Role Problems   ## Coding

1. Social role _____   _ _XX.XXX
   Type _____   XX_ _.XXX
   Severity _____   XXXX._XX
   Duration _____   XXXX.X_X
   Coping ability _____   XXXX.XX_

   Coding summary   _ _ _ _ _._ _ _

2. Social role _____   _ _XX.XXX
   Type _____   XX_ _.XXX
   Severity _____   XXXX._XX
   Duration _____   XXXX.X_X
   Coping ability _____   XXXX.XX_

   Coding summary   _ _ _ _ _._ _ _

3. Social role _____   _ _XX.XXX
   Type _____   XX_ _.XXX
   Severity _____   XXXX._XX
   Duration _____   XXXX.X_X
   Coping ability _____   XXXX.XX_

   Coding summary   _ _ _ _ _._ _ _

Factor II   Environmental Problems

1. Social system _____   _ _XXX.XX
   Subcategory _____   X_XX.XX
   Problem _____   XX_ _.XX
   Severity _____   XXXX._X
   Duration _____   XXXX.X_

   Coding summary   _ _ _ _ _._ _

2. Social system _____   _ _XXX.XX
   Subcategory _____   X_XX.XX
   Problem _____   XX_ _.XX
   Severity _____   XXXX._X
   Duration _____   XXXX.X_

   Coding summary   _ _ _ _ _._ _

3. Social system _____   _ _XXX.XX
   Subcategory _____   X_XX.XX
   Problem _____   XX_ _.XX
   Severity _____   XXXX._X
   Duration _____   XXXX.X_

   Coding summary   _ _ _ _ _._ _

Summary of PIE Assessment

Case: _____   Evaluator: _____

Date: _____

Assessment Findings	Code	Recommended Interventions
Factor I Social Role		
1.		
2.		
3.		
Factor II Environmental		
1.		
2.		
3.		
Factor III Mental Health		
DSM-IV: Axis I		
DSM-IV: Axis II		
Factor IV Physical Health		
1.		
2.		
3.		

Appendix A

Training Social Workers in the Use of PIE

Since the early 1980s the coauthors have made numerous presentations and conducted training sessions on the person-in-environment (PIE) system to social work audiences throughout the United States. Most of these presentations and training sessions have taken place at National Association of Social Workers (NASW) chapter, regional, and national conferences; but many have also been conducted at social agencies such as Grady Memorial Hospital in Atlanta; the Family Service Association of America in Florida; United Charities in Chicago; the Los Angeles County–University of Southern California County Medical Center; the Commonwealth of Massachusetts Department of Mental Health; the New York State Psychiatric Institute; the Department of Psychiatry, Kaiser Permanente Medical Center, San Rafael, California; and Atascadero State Hospital in California.

These presentations have ranged from brief 20-minute overviews of PIE to 1½-day intensives to prepare social workers to use PIE in practice. The coauthors have conducted presentations as a team and also individually.

We have found that most social workers understand enough of the PIE system to begin to use it in their practice after eight hours of training. It is also our impression that social workers who are familiar with the use of the *Diagnostic and Statistical Manual of Mental Disorders, Fourth Edition* (DSM-IV) (American Psychiatric Association, 1994) or the *International Classification of Diseases–Ninth Revision–Clinical Modification* (ICD-9-CM) (U.S. Department of Health and Human Services, 1991) have an easier time learning PIE because of their familiarity with a multifactorial reporting system.

Exhibit 1 shows an outline of a typical eight-hour training format the authors use to introduce social workers to PIE.

Preworkshop Preparation

A seminar or workshop on the PIE system can take place under a number of auspices: a regional NASW meeting, an annual chapter conference, a national NASW conference, or a gathering of social workers from a large agency or a group of smaller agencies. Although a homogeneous training group has the advantage of being able to focus on the use of PIE in a particular social work setting or with a particular group of clients, it is possible to train social workers from varied settings in the same training workshop. There is some advantage to a more heterogeneous training group because social workers learn that PIE is not limited to use in a particular social work setting but encompasses all practice settings.

Exhibit 1

A Model One-Day Workshop Outline

8:30 AM	Reception
9:00	Introduction
	Review of workshop goals and format
9:15	Origins and purposes of the PIE system
9:30	Factor I and Factor II
10:30	Break
10:45	Factor III and Factor IV
	Coding system
11:00	Walk-through of a case: The case of Jean
11:30	Discussion
12:00 PM	Lunch
1:00	First video case assessment
2:00	Second video case assessment
3:00	Break
3:15	Discussion
	Using PIE with a case presented by a trainee
3:45	Final questions, discussion, critique of PIE and workshop

Because PIE is not yet in use as the standard classification system for social work and because of the limited time available for most social workers to attend training seminars, strong management support for attendance will help ensure a cadre of enthusiastic participants. Providing a copy of a brief article on PIE (Karls & Wandrei, 1992a; 1992b; Williams, Karls, & Wandrei, 1989) may also be useful to pique interest. Once exposed to PIE, most trainees find it immediately relevant and useful for their social work practice.

We have provided training sessions for as few as five or six social workers and for as many as 50. Generally, the smaller the group the more quickly and thoroughly the material is learned and applied.

Seven types of materials are needed for the training sessions:

1. A copy of the *PIE Manual* for each participant
2. Two or three rating forms for each participant (from the *PIE Manual*)
3. A copy of the Mini-PIE for each participant (from the *PIE Manual*)
4. Videotaped case material including at least two vignettes with adults (such as the DSM Training Tapes [Reid, 1989] or other videotaped case material from a school of social work)
5. Video monitors
6. Several copies of DSM-IV for reference purposes
7. Blackboard or large pad of paper

We have experimented with providing trainees with the *PIE Manual* before the training session, but have found that most social workers are too busy to read the material until the training has started. We now distribute this material at the training session.

We have had great difficulty finding videotaped case material that is relevant to social work assessment and appropriate for our training needs. We have often used the training tape developed for DSM-III-R (Reid, 1989), because these vignettes are clear and professionally done, although their focus is on diagnosing mental disorder. However, there is seldom much information presented in these vignettes for evaluating the presence of environmental problems so we have sometimes supplemented the videotaped information with additional case material. For example, the first case on the training tape is a depressed woman who feels overwhelmed since her husband got a promotion and now travels a great deal. There are no obvious environmental problems in the vignette. Workshop attendees are told that in addition to the problems presented on the tape, this client does not feel safe in her neighborhood because of burglaries that have occurred in the past two months and because the police department is slow to respond to calls for assistance.

We have developed our own PIE training tape using videotaped case material obtained primarily from the University of California, Berkeley, School of Social Welfare, and the University of Southern California School of Social Work. However, the technical quality of these tapes has often been poor, and there is seldom much information pertaining to social role and environmental problems presented in the vignettes. A professionally made, high-quality training tape is needed for specific use in the PIE training, but the high cost of producing such a tape has prevented us from developing one.

Workshop Activities

We begin the workshop by introducing ourselves, including our professional background, and our experience with the PIE system. We ask workshop participants to briefly introduce themselves, their work setting, and their familiarity with PIE. However, it is important not to use a great deal of valuable workshop time doing extensive introductions.

We give an overview of what the training will involve. We explain that this is a workshop that builds on itself. Therefore, it does not work for participants to attend only part of the workshop or to leave early.

We begin by doing a didactic presentation outlining the origins and purposes of the PIE system. We highlight some of PIE's major features, for example, that it is multifactorial, that it focuses on adults, and that is meant for use in all social work settings by practitioners with different theoretical orientations.

We then describe Factor I (see chapter 2 of the book *Person-in-Environment System* for a basic description of the structure of the PIE system) using the blackboard or paper pad to illustrate how the parts of a Factor I description fall together. We define what a social functioning problem is and discuss the four subcategories of social functioning problems, illustrating each by reading a sample social role description from the *PIE Manual*. We stress the normative nature of the PIE social functioning problems (how nonpathologizing it is, for example, to have a Parent Role Problem) and the need to take into account the cultural and social context in evaluating a client's social functioning problem.

We describe the types of social role problems, again reading an example from the *PIE Manual*. We then explain the Severity, Coping, and Duration Indexes and demonstrate how they are used to modify the social role problem listing.

We follow this same procedure with Factor II. We discuss the six sub-groups of environmental problems and highlight how PIE allows social workers to record how environmental factors affect a client's social role problems. We stress that environmental problems arise outside of the client but affect the client's social functioning problems. We describe the use of the Severity and Duration indexes with the environmental problems, and again we use the blackboard or paper pad to illustrate how the elements of environmental problems build on each other and affect the client's behavior.

Because Factors I and II are at the core of the PIE system, we allow time for this new material to be digested, including a discussion of questions from the trainees and breaks as necessary. We then describe how DSM-IV's Axis I and II are incorporated into Factor III and how ICD-9-CM is incorporated into Factor IV. We do not spend a great deal of time on DSM-IV or ICD-9-CM because separate training is needed to acquire a thorough working knowledge of these systems.

We explain that there is a numerical coding system that can be used along with or instead of the descriptors. We stress that it is not important to learn this numerical system because it is readily available in the manual.

After we have presented all four factors and the three modifying indexes, we use the following case to demonstrate recording a client's problems according to the PIE system. We use a case specific to the particular setting if we are training a homogeneous group, drawing on case examples from the different social practice settings in the *PIE Manual*.

Case Study

Jean is a 23-year-old single mother of two preschool-age children who visits her local community mental health clinic at the suggestion of a friend who had received help there. Jean tells the intake social worker that for the past two years she has been worried about her ability to be a good enough parent for her children. In the past, Jean has had some problems acting independently as a parent, but she has been able to solve most parenting problems. She loves her children and wants them to have a better life than she had growing up. She does well at her low-paying job in a factory, the only kind of work available in her community for the past three years. When she returns home from work each evening after picking up her children from a friend's house, she is afraid that she "tunes out" her children and becomes inattentive to their needs. Until three weeks ago she was barely able to make ends meet, but now, with an increase in rent, she can't see how she can provide for herself and her children. Rents in her community have escalated dramatically in the past 10 months.

A secondary concern is Jean's relationship with her boyfriend, Mike, who is very much in love with her. For the past three months she has wondered whether she wants to continue seeing him. He's nice enough, and she enjoys seeing him, but he's not the "love of her life." She doesn't want to hurt his feelings so she continues to see him.

Jean reports that all of these concerns have made her feel very confused and depressed. She keeps breaking into tears, can't sleep, and barely has enough energy to get through the day. She's thought about taking her own life. She has also noticed that her asthma, which hadn't bothered her for several years, has been getting worse lately.

Information is elicited from the trainees by asking them questions about what they think Jean's primary social role problem is. We then go through recording on each of the four factors, although we spend very little time recording on Factors III and IV. We do not go into recording the numerical codes at this time because trainees find this confusing at this early point. When we record each element of each factor, we add it to our PIE listing on the blackboard or paper pad until we end up with a complete PIE statement on Jean (Exhibit 2).

We ask that the trainees compare the PIE statement with the DSM-IV statement for this client (Exhibit 3). We suggest that the PIE statement gives a much fuller picture of this client's problems than DSM-IV, and that PIE identifies the areas where social work intervention is immediately needed. We suggest how easy it is once a PIE statement is completed on a client to go through each problem listed and develop possible interventions.

In the next training segment we show the trainees a videotaped assessment interview. Vignettes should be from 10 to 20 minutes long. They can be tailored to the specific needs of each group. If we have a heterogeneous group, we often use the vignette on the DSM training tape of a severely depressed woman with marital problems. We suggest that the trainees use the Factor I and Factor II Worksheet in this manual (chapter 7) to keep track of their impressions while viewing the videotape. At this point we still do not emphasize the use of the numerical codes. After viewing the tape, we ask the group to break up into groups of two or three to work on developing the PIE statement together. We ask them to record the results of their assessment on the Summary of PIE Assessment form found in this manual (chapter 7). This process typically takes 30 minutes. We make ourselves available for consultation to the small groups. We then share the results of the ratings from each small group with the entire group, using the blackboard or paper pad. Most often there is a fairly high degree of consensus on the number and types of social functioning and environmental problems.

In the next segment, we present another videotape and go through the

Exhibit 2

Jean's PIE Assessment

Factor I	1130.324	Parent Role Problem, responsibility type, moderate severity, one to five years' duration, somewhat inadequate coping skills (presenting problem)
	2120.244	Lover Role Problem, ambivalence type, low severity, one to six months' duration, somewhat inadequate coping skills
Factor II	5401.42	Economic/Basic Needs System Problem, insufficient economic resources in community to provide sustenance for client and dependents, high severity, one to five years' duration
	5203.33	Economic/Basic Needs System Problem, shelter, other shelter problem (unavailability of affordable housing), moderate severity, six months' to one year's duration
Factor III		
Axis I	296.22	Major Depression, single episode, moderate severity
Axis II		No diagnosis
Factor IV	V71.09	Asthma (by client report)

Exhibit 3
Jean's DSM-IV Assessment

Axis I	296.22	Major Depression, single episode, moderate severity
Axis II	V71.09	No diagnosis
Axis III		Asthma (by client statement)
Axis IV	V61.2	Parent–Child Problem (parenting)
	V61.9	Adult Problem (relationship with boyfriend)
	V60.9	Housing Problems (lack of affordable housing)
	V60.9	Economic Problems (inadequate income)
Axis V	GAF = 70	

NOTE: GAF = Global Assessment of Functioning.

same process. This time we suggest that the participants try to use the numerical codes. Typically, this process is much faster the second time and there is greater consensus in the ratings. If time allows, we ask someone to present a case out of their own practice and to go through the process of doing a PIE statement.

We allow time for final discussion, questions, and ask for written feedback about both the usefulness of PIE and the training format.

Conclusion

Our experience has been that after eight hours of training, most social workers acquire enough basic information to begin to use PIE effectively in their daily practice. When questions not addressed in the training arise, the *PIE Manual* can be used to answer them. As PIE is used regularly, the time required to do a PIE statement becomes shorter. This process should be even faster once PIE is computerized (see chapter 16 of the book *Person-in-Environment System*). To reinforce the training, it is desirable to have a review session with the trainees a month or two after the initial training.

References

American Psychiatric Association. (1994). *Diagnostic and statistical manual of mental disorders* (4th ed.). Washington, DC: American Psychiatric Press.

Karls, J. & Wandrei, K. (1992a). The person-in-environment system for classifying client problems: A new tool for more effective case management. *Journal of Case Management, 1,* 90–95.

Karls, J., & Wandrei, K. (1992b). PIE: A new language for social work. *Social Work, 37,* 80–85.

Reid, W. (1989). *The DSM-III-R clinical vignettes.* New York: Brunner-Mazel.

U.S. Department of Health and Human Services. (1991). *International classification of diseases–9th revision–clinical modification* (4th ed.). Washington, DC: U.S. Government Printing Office.

Williams, J.B.W., Karls, J., & Wandrei, K. (1989). The person-in-environment (PIE) system for describing problems of social functioning. *Hospital and Community Psychiatry 40,* 1125–1126.

Appendix B

Social Work Interventions

The following is a list of common social work interventions that can be used for treatment planning once a PIE assessment is completed. The interventions are arbitrarily divided into three groups, one that targets interpersonal problems, one that targets environmental problems, and one that targets intrapersonal problems. The terms used to describe the interventions are taken from social work literature (mostly from *The Social Work Dictionary* [Barker, 1991]) and are not defined. Some of the terms overlap; they repeat other listings and could be listed in several different categories. Some terms are derived from treatment theories and some reflect techniques used in these treatment theories. This list is not exhaustive. There are other interventions that could be added.

Interventions Targeting Interpersonal Problems

Assertiveness training
Audio or video feedback
Aversion therapy
Behavior therapy
Behavioral family therapy
Behavioral modification
Behavioral rehearsal
Bibliotherapy
Brief therapy
Career counseling
Case management
Client-centered (Rogerian) therapy
Collaborative therapy
Communication training
Conciliation
Concurrent therapy
Confrontation and interpretation
Conjoint therapy
Counseling
Counseling, group therapy
Crisis intervention
Direct advice
Divorce therapy
Education
Ego supportive casework

Family life education
Family therapy
Feminist therapy
Financial management
Foster care (adult and child)
Genetic counseling
Grief work
Marital therapy
Marriage counseling
Mediation
Milieu therapy
Modeling
Modifying attribution
Multiple impact therapy
Mutual help group
Negative reinforcement
Network therapy
Parent training
Participant modeling
Play therapy
Positive reinforcement
Prayer/spiritual counseling
Problem-solving casework
Protective custody
Protective service

Psychodrama
Psychosocial casework
Rational casework
Reinforcement/behavioral
    modification
Role playing
Self-help group
Separation
Sex education
Sex therapy
Sibling therapy

Social skills training
Strategic family therapy
Structural family therapy
Supportive counseling
Task assignment
Task-centered approach
Task-centered problem solving
Transactional analysis
Ventilation
Vocational guidance
Vocational rehabilitation

Interventions Targeting Environmental Problems

Active resistance
Bargaining
Boycott
Case advocacy
Client advocacy
Community-based social action
Confrontation
Consultation
Cooptation
Day care
Developing therapeutic milieu
Education of community or
    influentials

Forming alliances
Interpretation to community or
    influentials
Mediation
Negotiation
Networking
Ombudsperson intervention
Passive resistance
Placement facilitation
Political action
Use of influentials
Use of mass media

Interventions Targeting Intrapersonal/Intrapsychic Problems

Behavior modification
Cognitive therapy
Existential therapy
Family therapy
Feminist therapy
Gestalt therapy
Group therapy
Guided imagery
Hypnotherapy
Imagery relaxation therapy
Implosive therapy
Individual psychotherapy (psycho-
    dynamic, Gestalt, psychoanalytic,
    Jungian, Adlerian, and so on)

Inpatient treatment/hospitalization
Logotherapy
Peer confrontation group
Peer support group
Primal therapy
Psychoanalysis
Psychodrama
Psychotropic medications
Rational emotive therapy
Reality therapy
Residential treatment
Role playing
Spiritual counseling
Transactional analysis

Reference

Barker, R. (1991). *The social work dictionary* (2nd ed.). Washington, DC: NASW Press.